Mallorca

W0384273

Schon immer war diese Insel anziehend: Die ersten Spuren menschlicher Siedlungen gehen auf die Zeit um 4000 v. Chr. zurück. Im Jahre 1230 eroberte der katalanische König Jaume der Erste die Insel. Heute ist Mallorca ein schnell zu erreichendes Ziel für Urlauber, Aus- und Umsteiger, Fincabesitzer, Sportler, Lebenskünstler, Prominente und solche, die es sein wollen.

A pair of osprey circles silently over the mountain peaks, down in the valley green almond tree plantations grow above the red soil, the sun burns hot and delicious island wine runs down one's throat. There are only 60 kilometres between the hiking group in the quiet of the monastery mountain "Puig de Maria" high above Pollença in the north of Mallorca and the beer-drinking guys on the Playa de Palma. Those are 60 kilometres which separate worlds. But the one as the other both belong to Mallorca.There is the capital of Palma, there is one of the most breathtaking dream roads in Europe winding from Formentor to Andratx through the high mountains in the west, in the east one little turquoise bathing cove surpasses the other, hidden hermitages and caves surprise the mountain hiker.
This island has always been attractive: the first traces of human settlements go back to the time about 4000 BC. In 1230 the Catalan King Jaume I conquered the island. Today Mallorca is soon reached by holiday-makers, dropouts, people wanting a change, finca owners, sportsmen, people making the best out of life, prominent figures, and those who would like to be.

Palma | Am Hafen

1 Der Hafen von Palma ist die Seele der Stadt. Von hier aus wurde in den vergangenen Jahrhunderten Handel mit der ganzen Welt getrieben. Nun ist Palmas Hafen beileibe kein Relikt aus vergangenen, glorreichen Zeiten. Er hat nach wie vor eine große wirtschaftliche Bedeutung. Hier legen nicht nur zahlreiche Frachter an, sondern auch die großen Fähr- und Kreuzfahrtschiffe. Bisweilen scheint es, als habe das Meer eine riesige Insel angeschwemmt. Dann ist mal wieder ein US-Flugzeugträger in der Bucht von Palma vor Anker gegangen, und die amerikanischen Matrosen überfluten die Altstadt. Die Sportsektion ist einer der größten Jachthäfen des Mittelmeers, und noch immer liefern einheimische Fischkutter ihren frischen Fang an der Fischermole ab. Dort sortieren und flicken die Fischer ihre Netze – ein beliebtes Fotomotiv für Touristen. An der gegenüber gelegenen Mole kann man Frischfisch kosten. Eine delikate Spezialität ist lubina (Wolfsbarsch) in der Salzkruste. Außerdem gibt es in Ciutat Jardí, Palmas östlicher Vorstadt am Meer, eine wunderbare Fressmeile im Carrer Illa de Xipre nur für Fisch und Meeresfrüchte.

At the harbour

Palma's harbour is the soul of the city. Over the course of the centuries trade was carried out from here all over the world. But Palma's harbour is certainly no mere relic of past glorious days. It is still of great economic importance. Not only do numerous freighters moor here, but also large ferry-boats and cruisers. Sometimes it seems as though the sea had washed up a huge island. Then a US aircraft-carrier drops anchor in the Bay of Palma and the American sailors swamp the old town. The sport section is one of the largest marinas in the Mediterranean, and local trawlers still deliver their fresh catch at the harbour mole. The fishermen sort the fish and repair their nets there – a favourite photo motiv for tourists. On the opposite mole you can taste the fresh fish. A delicious speciality: lubina (wolf perch) in a salt crust. In Ciutat Jardi, Palma's eastern suburb at the sea, there is also a wonderful food mile in the Carrer Illa de Xipre only for fish and seafood.

Inhalt · Contents

Mallorca

42 Freizeit-Tipps
Tips for your leisure time

Über dem Berggipfel kreist lautlos ein Fischadlerpärchen, ganz unten im Tal grünen Mandelbaum-Plantagen über der roten Erde, die Sonne brennt heiß und köstlicher Inselwein rinnt durch die Kehle. Nur 60 Kilometer liegen zwischen der Wandergruppe in der Stille des Klosterberges "Puig de Maria" hoch über Pollenca im Norden Mallorcas und den bierseligen Ballermännern an der Playa de Palma. Es sind 60 Kilometer, die Welten trennen. Aber die eine wie die andere gehört zu Mallorca. Da ist die Hauptstadt Palma, da windet sich eine der atemberaubendsten Traumstraßen Europas von Formentor bis nach Andratx durchs Hochgebirge im wilden Westen, da übertrumpft im Osten eine kleine türkisblaue Badebucht die andere, da überraschen versteckte Einsiedeleien, Höhlen und Kohlenmeiler den Bergwanderer.

Palma |
Dem Mammon geweiht: Sa Llotja

2 Die Llotja ist ein Kleinod in der guten Stube von Palma – der Palmenallee am Passeig de Sagrera. Die Seehandelsbörse von Palma wurde 1426 bis 1451 von den Gebrüdern Guillermo und Miquel Sagrera errichtet; sie gilt als Meisterwerk des Baumeisters Guillermo Sagrera. Die Llotja war ein bedeutendes Machtzentrum des mediterranen Handels. Der wunderschöne Engel über dem Portal, Schutzheiliger der Kaufleute, veranlasste Carlos den Ersten bei seinem Besuch in Palma zu glauben, er stünde vor einer Kirche. Den eleganten, großen Innenraum zieren sechs spiralig gedrehte Säulen, die das Deckengewölbe tragen. Heute ist die historische Börse ein beliebtes Forum für Ausstellungen von alter und neuer Kunst. (Die Stadt informiert in ihrem Veranstaltungskalender.) Vor der Llotja stehen die eigentlichen Wahrzeichen der Stadt: Palmen in Reih und Glied. Sie spenden dem Spaziergänger Schatten und verleihen der Allee trotz des tosenden Verkehrs auf der Avinguda Gabriel Roca so etwas wie Frieden und Ruhe. Bereits die Römer gaben der Stadt den Namen dieser Baumart: Palmaria. Die Araber nannten sie Medina Mayurca und die christlichen Eroberer Ciudad (Stadt) de Mallorca. Erst im 16. Jahrhundert kam der alte Name Palma wieder auf und in Gebrauch. Als die Insel noch nicht so sehr erschlossen war, sprachen die Dörfler von ihrer "ciutat".

The maritime stock market La Llotja

The Llotja is a jewel in Palma's "showpiece" – the avenue of palm trees on the Passeig de Sagrera. Palma's maritime stock market was built between 1426 and 1451 and is a masterpiece of the master builder Guillermo Sagrera. The Llotja was an important centre of Mediterranean trade. The large elegant interior is decorated by six spiral columns. Today the stock market is a popular forum for exhibitions of ancient and modern art. (Information in the calendar of events.) The real landmarks of the town stand in front of the Llotja: palm trees in rank and file. They give shade to the stroller and convey a feeling of peace and quiet in spite of the traffic on the Avinguda Gabriel Roca. It was the Romans who first gave the town the name of this tree: Palmaria. The Arabs called it Medina Mayurca and the Christian conquerors Ciudad (town) de Mallorca. The old name of Palma was only reintroduced in the 16th C. When the island was not yet so well-develoved, the villagers still spoke of their "ciutat".

Kathedrale La Seo
Juni-Sept. Mo.-Fr. 10-18 Uhr,
April, Mai und Okt. 10-17.15 Uhr,
Nov.-März Mo.-Fr. 10-15.15 Uhr,
Sa. 10-14.15 Uhr

Palma | Das Königsgelübde aus Stein

3 Wie ein helles Gebirge erhebt sich die Kathedrale La Seo über dem Hafen von Palma – mächtig und filigran zugleich. Die Bischofskirche, die zu den fünf schönsten von Spanien gehört, ist der ganze Stolz der Mallorquiner. Ihren Bau verdankt die Insel einem königlichen Gelübde. 1229 war Jaime von Aragón aufgebrochen, um die Balearen von den Arabern zu befreien. Die Überfahrt stand unter einem denkbar schlechten Stern. Ein Sturm kam auf, als hätte ihn der maurische Wali von Palma beim Satan bestellt. König Jaime fürchtete um sein Leben, um seine Reiter und Rosse. In seiner Not flehte er die Muttergottes an und bat um ihren Beistand. Dann schwor er, dass er der Madonna eine stolze Kirche bauen werde, falls er Palma erobern könnte. Tatsächlich flaute der Sturm ab, und am Silvestertag zog der siegreiche Jaime in der Stadt ein. Am Neujahrsmorgen 1230 ließ er in der Moschee von Palma das Kreuz aufstellen. Kurze Zeit später begann der Kirchenbau, der erst 1604 beendet war. Durch eine Rosette (Durchmesser über elf Meter), die aus 1236 einzelnen farbigen Glasteilen besteht, fällt das Tageslicht ein und verzaubert das Kircheninnere. Die letzten baulichen Veränderungen schuf der Katalane Antoni Gaudí mit seinem überdimensionalen Altarleuchter und gegenwärtig ist es der Mallorquiner Miguel Barceló, der mit einem riesigen Keramik-Relief in der Kapelle des Heiligen Petrus die Speisung der Zehntausend darstellt.

A kings's vow in stone

The cathedral La Seo rises like a bright mountain over the harbour of Palma – mighty and yet filigreed. The bishop's church, one of the five most beautiful in Spain, is the pride and joy of the Mallorcans. It owes its construction to a kings's vow. In 1229 Jaime of Aragon set out to free the Balearic Islands from the Arabs. The crossing was ill-fated. A storm sprang up as if the Moorish Wali of Palma had ordered it from Satan. King Jaime feared for his life, his knights and horses. At that perilous juncture he prayed to the Mother of God for help. He swore that he would build the Madonna a beautiful church if he could conquer Palma. The storm subsided and on New Year's Eve the victorious Jaime entered the town. On New Year's Day 1230 he had the cross erected in the mosque of Palma. A short time later the building of the church began, which was only completed in 1604. Daylight falls through a huge rose-window (over 11 m circumference) consisting of 1,236 coloured glass pieces and transforms the interior of the church.

Palma | Ansichts-Sache per Bus oder Kutsche

4 Die Polizei in Palma ist gnadenlos. Wer ohne Ticket (blaue Automaten) in den blau markierten Zonen der Innenstadt parkt, erhält eine multa (teure Strafgebühren) oder wird abgeschleppt. Die Tiefgaragen sind oft überfüllt und teuer. Empfehlenswert ist die Busfahrt nach Palma, zumal die Treppengassen und Fußgängerzonen viel besser zu Fuß zu meistern sind. Die doppelstöckigen, roten Busse der Linie 50 verbinden alle touristisch wichtigen Punkte der Stadt; über Kopfhörer gibt es Erklärungen – auch in Deutsch. Oder Sie mieten sich unterhalb der Kathedrale eine der roten galeras (Pferdekutschen); der Fiaker fährt durch die engen Altstadtgassen und weist auf die wichtigsten Bauten, Straßen und Plätze hin. Dazu zählen der Passeig des Born und der Passeig de la Rambla, zwei platanenüberdachte Flaniermeilen, der Passeig de Sagrera und Marítim, die palmengesäumten Hafenboulevards, prächtige Jugendstilfassaden wie das Gran Hotel und einige der vielen palaus (Altstadtpaläste), deren schmucke Innenhöfe jedoch leider meist verschlossen sind. Zu Füßen der Kathedrale und der Almudaina werden Sie wieder abgesetzt. In der Almudaina residierten einst die maurischen Herrscher der Balearen, später die mallorquinischen Könige. Weht über ihr die spanische Flagge, weilt König Juan Carlos I. auf Mallorca.

A carriage ride

The Palma police are merciless. Whoever parks without a ticket (blue machines) in the Blue Zones of the town centre, receives a multa (expensive fines) or is towed away. The underground car parks are often overcrowded and expensive. It is recommended that you take a bus to Palma, especially as the streets with steps and the pedestrian zones are much better on foot. Or below the cathedral you hire one of the red galleras, horse-drawn carriages: for three quarters of an hour and at a cost of 60,000 pts the driver takes you through the narrow streets of the old town and shows you the most important buildings and squares. Some of them are the Passeig des Born and the Passeig de la Rambla, two plane tree-lined avenues, the Passeig de Sagrera and Maritim, the palm tree-lined harbour boulevards, splendid art nouveau façades like the Grand Hotel and some of the many palaus, old town palaces, whose decorative inner courtyards are however unfortunately mostly closed. At the foot of the cathedral and the Almudaina you are set down once more. The Moorish rulers of the Balearics used to reside in the Almudaina, and later the Mallorcan kings.

Kreuzgang
Kloster Sant Francesc
Mo.-Sa. 9.30-12.30,
15.30-18 Uhr,
So. 9.30-12.30 Uhr

Palma | Wiege einer Weltstadt

5 Ein Traum in mediterraner Gotik ist der Kreuzgang des Klosters Sant Francesc. Kirche und Abtei gehören zu den bedeutendsten Sakralbauten der Stadt. Sant Francesc wurde 1232 von König Jaime von Aragón auf den Grundmauern einer Moschee gegründet. Hier lernten und lehrten die bedeutendsten Männer der mallorquinischen Geistesgeschichte. Ramón Llull zog von hier aus als Missionar in die arabische Welt und starb als Märtyrer. Sein Grabmal steht hinter dem Hauptaltar der Klosterkirche. Vor dem Gotteshaus erhebt sich das Bronze-Standbild des Fray Juníper Serra. Er war Padre aus dem kleinen Ort Petra. 1747 trieb es ihn in die Neue Welt. Er landete zunächst in Mexiko. Auf dem Weg nach Kalifornien gründete er 24 Missionsstationen. Eine davon nannte er nach seinem Orden Sant Francesc. Daraus entwickelte sich eine der schönsten Städte der Welt. Das schön restaurierte Arkadengeviert der Abtei an der Plaça Sant Francesc ist der größte gotische Kreuzgang in Europa – und gleichzeitig der lebendigste. Er dient den Schülern des Klostergymnasiums als Pausenhof und Stadtbesuchern und Einheimischen als stille Oase im Großstadttrubel.

Cradle of a cosmopolitan city

A dream in Mediterranean Gothic: the cloister of Sant Francesc Monastery. Church and abbey are two of the most important religious buildings in the town. Sant Francesc was built in 1232 by King Jaime of Aragon on the foundations of a mosque. It was here that the most important men of Mallorcan intellectual history learned and taught. Ramón Llull left from here to be a missionary in the Arabian world and died as a martyr. His gravestone stands behind the main altar in the monastery church. In front of the church stands the bronze statue of Fray Juníper Serra, a padre from the small village of Petra. In 1747 he set off to the New World. First he landed in Mexico. On the way to California he founded 24 mission stations. He called one of them Sant Francesc in memory of the monastery in Palma. One of the most beautiful cities in the world developed from it. The beautifully restored arcade square of the abbey on the Plaça Sant Francesc is the largest Gothic cloister in Europe. During the day it serves the pupils of the monastery high school as a school yard, in the evening religious music enhances the magnificent square.

Palma | Das Abaco

6 Eine simple, schwere Holztür in der Carrer Sant Joan 1 ist die Pforte in eine andere Welt. Wer die massive Tür des alten Herrschaftshauses hinter sich zuschlägt, betritt eine Kulisse, wie sie auch in einem Visconti-Film nicht märchenhafter ausgeschmückt ist. Wir stehen in der Empfangshalle des Stadtpalastes: Samtvorhänge, fantastische Blumenarrangements, ein gewaltiger Kamin, aus dem zuweilen ein dezenter Duft von Weihrauch strömt, Hunderte von brennenden Kerzen, Gemälde, Kupferstiche und Berge von exotischem Obst, wie aus einem Füllhorn über die Steinfliesen gekippt. Dazu klassische Musik, die aus allen Ecken strömt. Ein überwältigender Eindruck. Sie sind zu Gast in einem der schönsten Nachtclubs der Welt, in dem an und für sich gar nichts passiert, außer dass es um Mitternacht Blüten regnet. Man sitzt nur da, in der Palasthalle oder im kerzenbeschienenen Innenhof, lauscht der Musik und staunt. Fotografieren ist streng verboten wie auch in der riesigen Abaco-Filiale "Abacanto" am Stadtrand Richtung Inca (Ausfahrt Son Cladera), einem Landsitz mit Terrassen, Garten und Wasserspielen und unendlich viel neubarockem Dekor.

The Abaco

A simple heavy wooden door in Carrer Sant Joan is the gateway to another world. When you close the massive door of the old manor house you enter a fantastic scenario which couldn't be more fantastically decorated in a Visconti film. We are in the reception hall of the town palazzo: velvet curtains, magnificent flower arrangements, a huge fireplace from which a mild fragrance of incense streams. Hundreds of burning candles, paintings, copperplate engravings and mountains of exotic fruit as if tipped out of a horn of plenty. Classical music is everywhere to be heard. An overwhelming impression. You are a guest in one of the most beautiful nightclubs in the world, where basically nothing happens, except that at midnight it rains blossoms. One just sits there, in the palazzo hall or in the candle-lit inner courtyard, listens to the music and is amazed. Strictly no photographing, which also applies to the Abaco branch "Abacanto" on the outskirts of town in the direction of Inca (exit Son Cladera), a manor house with terraces, gardens and fountains and endless Baroque decoration.

Palma | Genialer Mix von Mittelalter und Moderne

7 Geradezu vorbildlich fügt sich das 2004 eröffnete "Museo d'art modern i contemporani" in die historische Festungsanlage "Es Baluard" ein. Ein moderner, sehr heller Bau aus Stahl, Beton, Glas, der immer wieder Einblicke zu den wehrhaften Steinquadern der ehemaligen Stadtmauer gestattet. Sowohl vom riesigen Innenhof als auch von den diversen Dachterrassen hat der Besucher ganz neue, sehr eindrucksvolle Aussichten auf Hafen und Kathedrale. In seinem Innern ist zeitgenössische spanische und internationale Kunst zu sehen. Eine gesonderte Abteilung wurde Malern gewidmet, die in unserem und im 20. Jahrhundert auf Mallorca wirkten – allen voran die Künstler der sogenannten "Schule von Pollenca", die sich um den katalanischen Jugendstil-Maler Hermengildo Anglada Camarasa scharten. Die boveda, ein Gewölbe im Kellergeschoss des Museums, eignet sich hervorragend für Werke von Performance-Künstlern, die mit den unterschiedlichsten Medien spielen.

"Es Baluard"
Sommer:
Di.-So. 10-24 Uhr,
Winter:
Di.-So. 10-20 Uhr

Brilliant mixture of middle ages and modern art

The "Museo d'art modern I contemporani", which was opened in 2004, fits perfectly into the historical fortress "Es Baluard". It is a modern, very light building made of steel, concrete and glass which repeatedly affords views of the well-fortified stone blocks of the former town wall. The visitor gets quite new impressive views of the harbour and cathedral from the huge inner courtyard as well as from the various roof terraces. In the interior, contemporary Spanish and international art can be seen. A special department is dedicated to artists who worked on Mallorca in ours and the 20th century – above all, the artists of the so-called "School of Pollença", who gathered around the Catalan art nouveau artist Hermengildo Anglada Camarasa. The "boveda", a vault in the cellar of the museum, is extremely fitting for works of performance-artists who play with the most varied media.

Palma | Ein Schloss voll Lust und Leid

8 "Castell de Bellver" – Schloss zur schönen Aussicht. Ein treffender Name. Der elegante, turmbewehrte Bau auf einem Hügel am Westrand der Stadt perfektioniert die Skyline Palmas. Und von seinen Zinnen hat man einen herrlichen Rundblick über Stadt, Altstadt und Hafen. Der Bau der Königsburg wurde 1309 unter Jaime II. beendet. Hier oben lag den Majestäten die Stadt zu Füßen, und sie genossen ihre Macht und ihr Reich. Leider ging es nicht allen Bewohnern des Castillo Bellver so. In den vergangenen Jahrhunderten war es sogar ein recht finsterer Ort, denn hier hatte Spanien eines seiner gefürchteten Gefängnisse für jeweils Andersdenkende untergebracht. Die ehemaligen Kerker wurden zum Historischen Museum der Stadt Palma, im kreisrunden Innenhof erklingt Sommernachtsmusik. Die Auffahrt ist vom Stadtteil El Terreno ausgeschildert.

In der Nähe (Cala Major, C/. Saridakis 29) befindet sich die Fundació de Pilar i Joan Miró. Sie erinnert an den katalanischen Maler Miró, der hier 40 Jahre bis zu seinem Tod 1983 lebte und arbeitete.

Historisches Museum der Stadt Palma
April, Mai, Juni, Sept.
tgl. 10-19 Uhr,
Juli + Aug.
tgl. 10-14, 16-21 Uhr,
Okt.-März
tgl. 10-17 Uhr

Fundació Pilar i Joan Miro
Sommer:
Di.-Sa. 10-19 Uhr,
So. + Fei. 10-15 Uhr,
Winter:
Di.-Sa. 10-18 Uhr,
So. + Fei. 10-15 Uhr

A castle full of love and sorrow

"Castell de Bellver" – the castle with a pleasant view. A fitting name. The elegant turreted building on a hill at the western edge of the city adds the finishing touch to Palma's skyline. And from its battlements you have a wonderful panoramic view over the city, old town and harbour. The royal castle was completed in 1309 under the rule of Jaime II. From up here the town lay at Their Majesties' feet and they enjoyed their power and their empire. During the past centuries it was actually a very sinister place, because Spain had one of its much-feared prisons for dissidents here. Unfortunately this didn't apply to all the inhabitants of the Castillo Bellver. The former dungeons were made into the Historical Museum of Palma, summer night's music plays in the circular inner courtyard. Drive up (signposted) from El Terreno.

Nearby (Cala Major, C/.Saridakis 29): the Fundació de Pilar i Joan Miró in memory of the Catalan artist who lived and worked here for forty years until his death in 1983.

Port de Portals | Der Seh-Hafen

9 Für Leute, die noch Illusionen oder (besser) Träume haben: In diesem Jachthafen, der als einer der exklusivsten des Mittelmeers gilt, ankert ein Luxusschiff neben dem anderen. Und dieser Anblick ist schon einen Besuch wert. 640 Liegeplätze – und alle sind höchstkarätig besetzt. Gelegentlich geht hier auch König Juan Carlos von Bord seiner "Fortuna". Gegen Abend pilgern Bootsbesitzer, schöne und junge Damen, die alle auf ihren Traumkapitän warten sowie jede Menge Schaulustige zur Restaurant-, Bar- und Boutiquenzeile vor den Anlegestegen: man sieht und wird gesehen. In noblen Restaurants, den Kunst- und Geldadel und die dicksten Jachten im Visier. Starköche zaubern wirklich Göttliches auf die Teller – zu ebensolchen Preisen. Aber selbst in diesem Hafen der Superlative müssen Besucher mit schmalem Geldbeutel nicht verhungern: Es gibt Restaurants, in denen sich junge Einheimische treffen und im bildschönen Terrassen-Café der "Cappuccino"-Kette kostet die Tasse café con leche auch nicht mehr als anderswo am Meer.

The marina of the multi-millionaires

For those who still have illusions or rather "dreams", in this plush marina, which is considered to be the most exclusive in the Mediterranean, one luxury ship is moored next to another. It is worth a visit just to see this: 640 berths, and all occupied by the best. Occasionally King Juan Carlos also leaves his "Fortuna" here. Towards evening, boat owners and beautiful young women in search of their dream captain, and lots of onlookers stroll along the jetty to the restaurants, bars and boutiques: one sees and is seen – in the noble restaurants, with the art and financial aristocracy and the biggest yachts in their sights. Star chefs conjure up divine dishes – and such are the prices. But even in this harbour of superlatives, visitors with only limited finances needn't go hungry: there are restaurants where young local people meet and in the lovely Terrace Café from the "Cappuccino" Chain, the cup of café con leche costs no more than elsewhere at the seaside.

Portals Vells | Der versteckte Strand

10 Ziemlich versteckt liegt die kleine Bucht im Südwesten der Insel, jenseits der Straße zum Cap de Cala Figuera. Trotz reger Bautätigkeit drumherum, lohnt der ausgeschilderte Weg dorthin. Die Bucht mit ihrem türkisfarbenen Wasser und goldgelbem Sandstrand wird von kleineren Felswänden gerahmt, so dass die Brandung nicht sehr stark ist. Das kommt ankernden Jachten, Schwimmern und Tauchern zugute. Hier wie auch in der benachbarten, fjordähnlichen Cala Figuera und in den meisten Buchten Mallorcas ist das Wasser kristallklar, ein ideales Tauchrevier. Eine faszinierende Unterwasserwelt tut sich Schnorchlern und Tauchern auf, mit zahlreichen Grotten, bizarren Korallenformationen, bunt schillernden Fischen und dem einen oder anderen Schiffswrack. Ähnlich wie in den Buchten der Cala Sant Vicenc im Norden und im Gebiet zwischen dem kleinen Badeort Sant Elm und der Insel Dragonera im äußersten Südwesten. Dort bietet die kleine Tauchbasis 'Scuba Activa' mit spanischen und deutschen Tauchlehrern Kurse für Anfänger- und Fortgeschrittene an; sie hat aber auch Höhlen- und Nachttauchgänge im Angebot.

The hidden beach

The small bay lies somewhat hidden in the southwest of the island, at the other side of the road to the Cap de Cala Figuera. In spite of a lot of building construction nearby, it is still worth making the signposted way there. The bay with its turquoise water and golden sands is protected by rocky cliffs, so the breakers aren't too strong. That is of benefit to the yachts lying at anchor there, and also to swimmers and divers. As with the neighbouring fjord-like Cala Figuera and most bays on Mallorca, the water is crystal clear, an ideal place for diving. Snorkellers and divers experience a fascinating underwater-world with numerous grottoes, bizarre coral formations, brightly shimmering fish and one or two shipwrecks. It is similar to the bays of Cala Sant Vicenc in the north, and to the area between the small bathing resort Sant Elm and the island Dragonera in the extreme southwest. There one can find the small diving centre 'Scuba Activa' where Spanish and German diving instructors give courses for beginners and experienced divers; it also offers cave and night diving.

Santa Ponça | Im Paradies der Golfer

11 Unter Kennern ist es kein Geheimnis: Mallorca ist ein wahres Golf-Paradies. Die kontrastreiche Insel bietet mit Meer, Gebirge und Ebene ein attraktives Umfeld. Von Palma, der Hauptstadt mit internationaler Gastronomie und regem Nachtleben, sind alle Plätze innerhalb einer Stunde erreichbar. 22 Plätze sind derzeit bespielbar, vier weitere befinden sich im Bau. Das Klima ist vor allem im Frühling, Herbst und Winter ideal; nahezu alle Plätze haben das ganze Jahr über geöffnet. Einer der schönsten ist "Golf Santa Ponça", die einzige 54-Loch-Anlage der Insel; allerdings sind nur 18 davon öffentlich, der Rest ist ausschließlich Club-Mitgliedern zugänglich. Am Ende der Runde durch eine relativ flache, von vielen Bäumen bewachsenen Landschaft, lockt der clubeigene Swimming-pool. Die vornehmste Anlage ist der edle "Son-Vida-Golfclub", eine 18-Loch-Anlage inmitten einer feinen Villengegend am Rande von Palma. Im "Son-Vida-Club" wurden wiederholt die "Open de Baleares" ausgetragen. Einer der neueren Plätze, er liegt auf der Halbinsel Alcanada bei Alcúdia, gehört zu den landschaftlich schönsten: 16 (!) der 18 Löcher und das Clubhaus mit gutem Restaurant haben Meerblick.

In a golfer's paradise

It's no secret among experts: Mallorca is a golfer's paradise. The island offers a variety of sea, mountains and plains – an attractive milieu. All golf courses can be reached within one hour of Palma; at the moment, 22 golf courses are open, four more are under construction. The climate is ideal, especially in spring, autumn and winter: nearly all the courses are open throughout the year. "Golf Santa Ponça" is one of the best, the only 54-hole course on the island. 18 holes are open to the public. The rest are for club members only. At the end of the course the Club's swimming-pool is situated in a relatively flat wooded landscape. The most distinguished golf course is the "Son-Vida-Golf Club" (18 holes) in the middle of a fine villa area on the outskirts of Palma. The "Open de Baleares" has repeatedly been held at the "Son-Vida-Club". One of the more recent golf courses is on the peninsula Alcanada near Alcúdia. It is also one of the most beautiful as far as scenery is concerned: 16 (!) of the 18 holes and the Club House with a good restaurant have a view of the sea.

Port d'Andratx | Sonnenuntergang am Meer

12 Zwei Wege führen zum Hafen von Andratx: der eine direkt vom Städtchen Andratx, der andere von Camp de Mar durch die Berge. Beide zeigen die ungeheuren Veränderungen, die die Gemeinde im Südwesten in den letzten Jahren erfahren hat. In die einstige Bilderbuchlandschaft kauften sich reiche Ausländer ein.So ist die einst abgeschiedene Felsbucht von Cala Llamp kein Badeversteck mehr. Im ehemaligen Fischernest Port d'Andratx hört man fast nur noch deutsche Laute, reihen sich Boutiquen, Immobilienbüros, Galerien deutscher Provenience aneinander. Dennoch lohnt ein Besuch dieses fast kreisrunden Naturhafens, besonders zur Abendzeit, wenn die Fischerboote heimkehren, wenn später die Sonne hinter dem Leuchturm im Meer versinkt. Zum Nobelhafen passen Luxusherbergen mit umwerfendem Hafenblick und teure Fischlokale mit romantischen Terrassen direkt am Meer.

Sunset over the sea

Two roads lead to Andratz: one directly from the village of Andratz, the other from Camp de Mar through the mountains. They both show the immense changes experienced by the community in the southwest over the past years. What was once a picture-book landscape has now been bought up by wealthy foreigners. And so the once secluded rocky bay of Cala Llamp is no longer a bathing hideaway. In the former fishing village Port d'Andratz almost only German can be heard, boutiques, estate agencies, and galleries of German provenience line up side by side. But it is still worth visiting this almost circular natural harbour, especially in the evening, when the fishing boats return and when later the sun disappears into the sea behind the lighthouse. Luxury accommodation with fantastic sea views and expensive fish restaurants with romantic terraces directly overlooking the sea go with the luxury harbour.

Sant Elm | Ende gut, alles gut

13 Auf Mallorca enden viele Straßen einfach am Meer. Fährt man nach Sant Elm, setzt wenigstens ein hübsches, altes Fischerdorf, das allerdings mit touristischer Infrastruktur "ausgestattet" wurde, dem Weg ein vergnügliches Ende. Sant Elm ist eine bekannte, muschelförmige Badebucht mit Sand- und Kieselstränden. Oft ankern hier Ausflugsschiffe, die ihre Passagiere zum Mittagessen entladen. Nach dem Essen bieten sich zwei Möglichkeiten an: Man könnte eine ausgedehnte Wanderung zum Trappistenkloster Sa Trapa nordöstlich von Sant Elm machen. (Hin- und Rückweg ca. zweieinhalb Stunden). Oder man lässt sich mit dem kleinen Fährboot "Margarita" in 20-minütiger Fahrt zur "Dracheninsel" Sa Dragonera übersetzen. Das Boot landet in der von Mallorca nicht einsehbaren ehemaligen Schmugglerbucht Cala Lladó. Dort hat jeder Dragonera-Gast einen Euro zu bezahlen, eine Art Ökosteuer für den Erhalt dieses weltabgelegenen Eilands, das 1995 zum "Parc Natural" erklärt wurde, nicht bebaut werden darf und von unzähligen endemischen Eidechsen (dragóns) und vielen Vogelarten, vornehmlich Möwen, bewohnt wird. Für Naturfreunde eine traumhafte Robinsonade!

All's well that ends well

Many roads on Mallorca just end at the sea. That's it! But if you drive to Sant Elm, a picturesque old fishing village, which has been somewhat "enriched" with touristic infrastructure, there is a pleasant end to the road. Sant Elm: a popular shell-shaped bay with sand and pebble beaches. Pleasure boats often moor here while their passengers have lunch. After lunch there are two possibilities: you could have a long walk to the Trappist Monastery Sa Trapa north-east of Sant Elm (about 2 1/2 hours there and back). Or you can take the little ferry-boat "Margarita" for a 20-minute crossing to the "dragon's island" Sa Dragonera. The boat lands in the unique hidden smugglers' bay Cala Lladó. There, every La Dragonera visitor has to pay one Euro, a sort of eco-tax for the preservation of this remote island which was made into a "Parc Natural" in 1995, must not be built on and is inhabited by countless endemic lizards (dragons) and many bird species, mainly seagulls. For nature lovers it is a fantastic "Robinsade"!

Galilea | Poesie eines Bergdorfes

14

Schon die Anreise macht Laune - falls man mit dem Auto kommt. Bei der Kirche von Capdella zeigt der Wegweiser in Richtung Norden. Fürwahr ein hübsches Tal. Etliche Radsportler haben für derlei Schönheit keinen Blick. Sie quälen sich mit roten Köpfen, denn die Straße führt stramm bergauf. Schließlich ist es geschafft. Unterhalb des Berges Galatzó schmiegt sich das Dorf Galilea in die Landschaft. Galilea? Richtig, der Ort wurde nach dem biblischen Dorf genannt; vielleicht weil er so abgeschieden liegt und einen so himmlischen Ausblick auf die Insel bietet. Man sollte ihn von der Terrasse der kleinen Kirche genießen. Das ist nun das andere Mallorca, das stille, das einfache. Touristentrubel und Betonsilos scheinen unendlich fern, kaum vorstellbar, dass 20 Kilometer weiter südlich die Hotelburgen von Tausenden von Urlaubern bevölkert werden. Galilea ist sich und seiner schlichten Schönheit treu geblieben. Auch wenn sich hier in den letzten 20 Jahren mehr und mehr Ausländer mit Zweitwohnsitz eingenistet haben. So auch ein amerikanisch-britisches Ehepaar, das eine kleine, romantische Hotelanlage hoch oben am Berg betreibt. Der Weitblick bis zum Meer ist im Preis inbegriffen. Mittelpunkt des Terrassendorfes ist der Kirchplatz mit einer einfachen Taverne, in der die Señora des Hauses gute tapas und einen jamón serrano (luftgetrockneten Schinken) serviert, der im Dorf seinesgleichen sucht.

The poetry of a mountain village

The journey there puts you in the right mood – if you arrive by car. The signpost near the church in Capdella directs you northwards. It really is a lovely valley. A great many cyclists however don't appreciate its beauty. They strain up the steep mountain with a great deal of stress. Then they've made it. The village of Galilea nestles in the landscape beneath Mount Galatzó. Galilea? Yes, the village was named after the biblical village – perhaps because it provides such a heavenly view over the island. Enjoy it from the terrace of the little church. This is a different Mallorca, a peaceful and simple one. Tourist bustle and concrete buildings seem to be very far away. It's hard to believe that just 20 km further south there are the high-rise hotels with thousands of holidaymakers. Galilea has remained faithful to its simple beauty. Some artists have settled here and pay their due to the landscape. But let's proceed to the little tavern next to the church. The señora serves ham here which is just as incomparable as the village itself.

La Reserva Galatzó / Parc Aventur | Kribbeln im Bauch

15 Einer der eindrucksvollsten Ferienparks auf Mallorca erstreckt sich über 2,5 Quadratkilometer bergiger Naturlandschaft unterhalb des 1026 Meter hohen Galatzó im Südwesten des Tramuntana-Gebirges. In diesem Park – im Reserva Galatzó – wurde auf sensible Weise der eh schon eindrucksvollen Natur nachgeholfen: Hier entdeckt der Besucher künstliche Wasserfälle, Höhlen und Teiche, die sich aus eigenen Quellen speisen, Vogelstimmen vom Band, Eulen-Volieren, Bärenzwinger und einen Grillplatz. Alte Köhler- und Kalkbrennerplätze wurden wieder hergerichtet und ein markierter Wanderpfad angelegt, der alle diese Verweilpunkte auf einer gut 90-minütigen Tour verbindet. Wer dann auch noch Abenteuerlust verspürt, kann den Parc Aventur unter gleicher Regie und auf demselben Gelände besuchen. Dieser Riesenspaß, der für Familien gedacht ist, verursacht bei dem einen oder anderen Besucher sicherlich Bauchkribbeln. Sei es beim Gang über eine schwankende Hängebrücke, bei der rasanen Talfahrt am Seil, beim Mountainclimbing in schwindelnder Höhe, beim Bogenschießen oder beim Mountainbike-Cross.

Butterflies in one's stomach

La Reserva Galatzó und Park Aventur
Sommer: tgl. 10-17 Uhr, Winter: tgl.10-16 Uhr

Probably the most successful holiday park of the island stretches over 2,5 square kilometres of mountainous countryside at the foot of the 1,026 m-high Galatzó in the southwest of the Tramuntana Mountains. This park has cleverly made use of the magnificent features of nature by adding artificial waterfalls, caves and ponds from real springs, with recorded birds' voices, aviaries with owls, a bear cage and a lovely barbecue area. Old charcoal ovens and limeworks have been restored and there is a signposted trail connecting all these places of interest in a 90-minute-tour. Those who still have an urge for adventure can visit the Parc Aventur, which is under the same management and on the same site. This park is suitable for families, and what might be great fun for some visitors can cause butterflies in other visitors' stomachs; for example, when walking over a swaying hanging bridge, whizzing down into the valley on a rope, mountain-climbing at a dizzy height, practising archery or mountain-biking.

Sa Granja | Herrensitz und Museum

16 Wer sich für Geschichte und Kultur Mallorcas interessiert, sollte Sa Granja unbedingt besuchen. Es ist ein typischer mallorquinischer Gutshof, wie es im Mittelalter viele gab. Bereits die Araber unterhielten hier ein Landgut, das nach der christlichen Rückeroberung in den Besitz von Zisterziensermönchen überging. Die Padres bauten die Anlage mit Handwerksbetrieben, Galerien um den Innenhof, Gärten und Parks aus. Heute ist das Gut das beliebteste Freiluftmuseum der Insel. Die meisten Gebäude sowie die Wasserspiele stammen aus dem 17. Jahrhundert. Jeden Mittwoch- und Freitagnachmittag kommt Leben in das Landgut: die Besucher können Handwerkern in ihren Originaltrachten beim Backen, Weben, Klöppeln, Schmieden und Töpfern zuschauen. Eine Trachtengruppe führt mallorquinische Tänze auf. Im Preis eingeschlossen sind Kostproben verschiedener regionaler Weinsorten und in Zucker oder Honig getauchte bunyols (Kartoffelteigkrapfen), die bis heute inseltypisch sind.

Sa Granja
Sommer:
tgl. 10-19 Uhr,
Winter:
tgl. 10-18 Uhr

Manor house and museum

Whoever is interested in the history and culture of Mallorca should definitely visit Sa Granja. It is a typical Mallorcan estate as could often be seen in the Middle Ages. The Arabs already had an estate here, and after the Christian conquest it went into the possession of the Cistercian monks. The padres extended the complex with workshops, galleries around the inner courtyard, gardens and parks. Today the estate is the most popular open-air museum on the island. Most of the buildings and the fountains originate from the 17th C. Every Wednesday and Friday afternoon the estate comes to life: the visitors can watch tradesmen in their traditional costumes baking, weaving, making bobbin-lace, working in a forge or in a pottery. A folklore group demonstrates Mallorcan dances. The programme always includes samples of various regional wines and sugared bunyols, potato dough fritters, which are still typical for the island today.

Torre de ses Ànimes | Turm der Ein- und Aussichten

17 Dieses historische Monument bietet einen ausgezeichneten Einblick in die mittelalterliche Geschichte Mallorcas: Kaum hatte König Jaime I. von Aragón die Insel den Arabern entrissen, drohte Gefahr von außen. Diesmal war es ein Christenbruder, der sich Mallorca einverleiben wollte: König Pedro von Aragón. Dann suchten Piraten die Küsten heim. Schließlich bedrohten im 15. Jahrhundert die Türken die Balearen. Die Bevölkerung lebte also in ständiger Angst vor Invasoren und schützte sich mit einer weitreichenden Rundumverteidigung. Man baute an der gesamten Küste auf den höchsten Erhebungen Wehrtürme, deren Besatzungen sich untereinander mit Rauch- und Feuerzeichen verständigen konnten, so dass im Falle eines Angriffs die Insel schnell alarmiert war. Der Torre de Ses Ànimes ist der wohl eindrucksvollste Zeuge jener bewegten Epoche Mallorcas. Heutzutage genießt man von hier oben ganz friedlich den herrlichen Ausblick auf die Nord- und Westküste. Die Sicht reicht bis zum Bergdorf Banyalbufar, inmitten von Terrassengärten gelegen. Es war einst ein arabischer Ort, der Bany-al-bahar hieß – kleiner Weingarten am Meer. Heute werden statt Weinstöcken Tomaten und andere Gemüsearten angebaut. Banyalbufar lebt jedoch von seinen Besuchern In den engen Treppengassen verstecken sich hübsche Tavernen und Restaurants. Die beiden felsenfesten Bergdörfer verbindet ein markierter Küstenwanderweg mit traumhaften Ausblicken aufs Meer.

Tower of insights and views

This historical monument offers an excellent insight into the medieval history of Mallorca: King Jaime I of Aragón had hardly won the island back from the Arabs when danger threatened from abroad. This time it was a fellow Christian who wanted to take Mallorca: King Pedro of Aragón. Then pirates attacked the coasts. Finally in the 15th C the Turks, who had just conquered Algeria, threatened the Balearic Islands. The inhabitants constantly lived in fear of invasion and protected themselves with an extensive defence system. All around the coast they built towers and the soldiers communicated with smoke and fire signals, so that alarm could be raised on the island as soon as there was an attack. The Torre de Ses Ànimes is probably the most impressive witness of that eventful epoch of Mallorca. Nowadays you can enjoy a wonderful view of the north and west coasts from up there. The view stretches to the wine village of Banyalbufar, situated in the middle of terraced gardens. It was once an Arabian village called Bany-al-bahar – meaning the little vineyard by the sea.

Valldemossa | Chopins Krankenlager

18 Dass es auf Mallorca bisweilen regnet, hatte man ihm verschwiegen. Zum Glück. Wer weiß, ob der Komponist Frédéric Chopin jemals das "Regentropfenprélude" geschrieben hätte. Das kränkelnde Musikgenie kam 1838 auf die Insel. Die Idee dazu hatte seine Geliebte George Sand, die die Freuden und Leiden dieses nasskalten Winteraufenthaltes in Palma und im Kloster von Valldemossa in Ihrem Buch "Ein Winter auf Mallorca"beschrieb.

Am Dorfeingang liegt das "Kulturzentrum Costa Nord", das einst Michael Douglas gehörte und das dieser 2003 an die Balearische Regierung verkaufte. Doch nach wie vor führt der amerikanische Hollywood-Star in einem Breitwand-Film und in mehreren Sprachen durch "sein" Mallorca, also die Küstenzone von Valldemossa bis Sóller, die auch Wahlheimat des habsburgischen Erzherzogs Ludwig Salvator (1847–1915) war. Dem hochbegabten Autor und Illustrator von über 70 Büchern, darunter einigen über die Balearen, widmet Douglas einen eigenen Schauraum: er ließ die Schiffskajüte von Ludwigs Jacht `Nixe´ nachbauen und erzählt dazu Legenden über dessen buntschillerndes Leben. Ein Hauch von Disneyland auf Mallorca.

Kartause von Valdemossa
Mo.-Sa.
9.30-13.30 Uhr,
15-18/19 Uhr

Kulturzentrum Costa Nord
Sommer: Mo.-Sa.
9.30-18.30 Uhr,
So. 10-13 Uhr,
Winter:
9.30-16/16.30 Uhr

Chopin's sick-bed

Nobody told him that it occasionally rained on Mallorca. Fortunately! Otherwise, who knows whether the composer Frédéric Chopin would ever have written his "Raindrop Prelude"? The ailing genius came to the island in 1838. It was the idea of his mistress, George Sand, who described the joys and sufferings of this wet-cold winter sojourn in Palma and in the Monastery of Valldemossa in her book "A Winter on Mallorca".

Michael Douglas's "Culture Centre Costa Nord" is situated at the entrance to the village. Accompanied by Hollywood choirs the American actor leads through "his" Mallorca in a wide-screen film and in several languages, that is, the coastal region from Valldemossa to Sóller, which was also the adopted place of residence of the Habsburg archduke Ludwig Salvator (1847–1915). Douglas dedicates a room to the highly talented author and illustrator of over 70 books, among them some about the Balearic Islands: he had the ship's cabin of Ludwig's yacht "Nixe" reconstructed and tells legends about his shimmering life.

Deià | Dorfschönheit

19 Dieses Dorf – einst weitgehend unbekannt – ist in seiner unverbauten Schönheit typisch für die Insel. Es liegt zu Füßen eines freistehenden Bergkegels. Zur kleinen, idyllischen, sommers jedoch überlaufenen Kiesbucht führt ein steiler Weg, den man nur teilweise mit dem Auto befahren kann. In Deià wurde die alte dörfliche Struktur bewahrt, allerdings nur rein äußerlich, denn der Ort ist das Dorf der oberen Zehntausend. Hier haben sich Wirtschaftsbosse und Filmstars, Künstler und Kaufleute niedergelassen, vorwiegend Millionäre. Die haben genug Geld, um alles picobello zu renovieren. Unter einer Bedingung: Man möchte unter sich bleiben, Ausflugsbusse dürfen hier nicht halten, und die Einheimischen haben auch nicht mehr viel zu melden. Mit dem englischen Schriftsteller Robert Ranke-Graves ("Ich, Claudius, Kaiser und Gott") begann der Boom. Er lebte und starb in Deià. Er wurde, wie so viele andere Künstler, auf dem kleinen romantischen Friedhof am Gipfel des Häuserberges begraben. Nach den Künstlern folgte der Geldadel. Trotz allem ist das schöne Deià einen Besuch wert – und sei es nur zum Geldausgeben, in den Boutiquen und Galerien oder in den vielen guten aber teuren Restaurants in denen Starköche kulinarische Wunder auf den Tisch bringen.

Village beauty

This village,which was once practically unknown, is typical of the island with its natural beauty. It is situated at the foot of an open mountain peak. The small, idyllic, but in summer overcrowded, stony bay can only be reached by a steep track which can only partly be driven along. The village structure has been retained in Deià, but only on the exterior, because this is the village of the élite of society. Big bosses and film stars (Michael Douglas), artists and businessmen have settled here. They have enough money to renovate everything immaculately. On one condition: they want to be left alone. No excursion buses are allowed to stop here and the local inhabitants don't have much say either. The boom began with the English author Robert Ranke-Graves ("I, Claudius, Emperor and God"). He lived and died in Deià. The financial aristocracy followed. But in spite of everything, pretty Deià is still worth visiting – and if only to spend money, in the boutiques and galleries and in the "El Olivo", the posh restaurant in the swish hotel "La Residencia".

Sóller | Unterwegs mit dem Roten Blitz

20 Der Vergleich mit dem Blitz ist natürlich liebevoll ironisch gemeint. Denn der "Ferrocarril de Sóller", also die berühmte Eisenbahn von Palma nach Sóller, ruckelt gemütlich durch Orangen- und Mandelhaine. 1912, als der Zug zum ersten Mal fuhr, kam das Tempo den Einheimischen blitzartig vor, denn seinerzeit pflegte man noch auf Maultierrücken und Eselskarren nach Sóller zu reisen. Fünfmal am Tag fährt der "Tren de Sóller" vom Bahnhof in Palma an der Plaça Espanya zum schönen Städtchen Sóller. Für die 27 Kilometer braucht er 40 Minuten ohne und 50 Minuten mit Fotostopp am Mirador del Pujol d'en Banya. Unterwegs hält er noch an den Bahnhöfen von Son Sardina und Bunyola. Im nostalgischen Jugendstil-Bahnhof von Sóller lohnt ein Blick in die kleine Boutique `Fet a Sóller´ mit hausgemachten Produkten aus dem Dorf.
Die schützenden Tausender ringsherum sind anstrengende aber lohnende Ziele für Bergwanderer. Seit die Eisenbahn 1997 Konkurrenz bekommen hat mit einem 3 km langen Straßentunnel (Mautgebühr) ist es mit Sóllers Weltabgeschiedenheit vorbei. Dennoch lohnt ein Besuch dieses Doppelortes mit dem quirligen Hafen und der nostalgischen Straßenbahn.

On the move with the Red Lightning

The comparison with lightning is, of course, meant in an affectionately ironic way. Bacause the "Ferrocarrill de Sóller", the famous railway from Palma to Sóller, travels slowly through orange and almond groves. In 1912, when the train started for the first time, the speed of it seemed to be like lightning to the local inhabitants who were only used to travelling to Sóller on the back of a mule or on a donkey-drawn cart. The "Tren de Sóller" leaves the station in Palma (Plaça Espanya) for the picturesque village five times a day. It takes 40 minutes for the 27 km, and 50 minutes with a photo stop at the Mirador del Pujol d'en Banya. It also stops at Son Sardina and Bunyola. In the nostalgic art nouveau station of Sóller it's worth visiting the little boutique "Fet a Sóller" with home-made products from the village. The protecting 1,000 m-high peaks around it are exhausting, but rewarding destinations for mountain hikers. Since the railway got competition in 1997 with a 3 km-long road tunnel (toll), Sóller is no longer an isolated village. But it is still worth visiting this twin village with its lively harbour and the nostalgic tram.

Alfabia | Die arabische Oase

21

Lieben Sie die Geschichten aus 1001 Nacht? Dann müssen Sie Alfabia besuchen und durch die duftenden Gärten des alten Arabiens lustwandeln: Stille Teiche spiegeln die Fächer der Palmen wider, Wasserspiele plätschern sanft und beflügeln die Fantasie – eine Oase der Muße und Ruhe. Fürst Benihabet, der maurische Statthalter von Inca, hat dieses Paradies, ein Beispiel arabischer Gartenbaukunst, anlegen lassen. Er war ein kluger Mann, der im Jahre 1229, nachdem König Jaime Palma erobert hatte, Kampfgefährte der aragonesischen Majestät wurde und zum Christentum übertrat. Das war ein weiser Entschluss, denn der dankbare Jaime schenkte ihm Alfabia, was ihm ja schon längst gehörte. Jedenfalls durfte der Araber seine Oase behalten. Das dazugehörige Schlösschen wurde im 17. Jahrhundert gebaut; es dient heute als Museum mit einer Sammlung an Möbeln, Teppichen, Stichen und alten Büchern. Eines der ganz wenigen, von den Christen nicht zerstörten arabischen Relikten ist in der Decke des Torturms zu bewundern: die prächtige Holztäfelung mit arabischen Schriftzeichen, die Allah preisen.

Landgut Alfabia
Mo.-Fr.
9.30-17.30 Uhr,
Sa. 9.30-13.30 Uhr

The Arabian oasis

Do you like the stories of Thousand and One Arabian Nights? Then you just have to visit Alfabia and walk through the scented gardens of old Arabia: smooth ponds reflect the palm fronds, fountains splash quietly and inspire the imagination – an oasis of musing and peace. Prince Benihabet, the Moorish governor of Inca, had this paradise made – an excellent example of Arabian landscape gardening. He was a clever man and after King Jaime had conquered Palma in 1229 he became a comrade in arms of the Aragon majesty and converted to Christianity. That was a wise decision because the grateful Jaime gave him Alfabia – which had already belonged to him for a long time. At any rate the Arab was allowed to keep the oasis. The little castle belonging to it was built in the 17th C; it is now a museum with a collection of furniture, carpets, engravings and old books.

Orient | Heitere Einöde

22 Ein stilles kleines Dorf in heiterer Einöde mit 10 (!) gemeldeten Einwohnern. So stellt man sich das Landleben auf Mallorca vor. Eine Handvoll Bruchsteinhäuser mit einer kleinen Kirche, umgeben von einem gigantischen Garten mit Weinstöcken, Zitrus- und Apfelhainen, Oliven- und Mandelbäumen. Es duftet nach Blumen und wilden Kräutern. Das ist auch wichtig, denn hier werden zum Teil die Pflanzen für den mallorquinischen Kräuterlikör Hierbas geerntet, der überall auf den Balearen getrunken wird. Man kann ihn in der Dorfbar kosten: süß für die Damen, herb für die Herren. Nach dem Apéritif geht's in die `L'Hermitage´, eine ehemalige, denkmalgeschützte Finca, in der einst erschöpfte Wandermönche verköstigt und beherbergt wurden. Die Gäste von heute werden verwöhnt, und zwar außergewöhnlich stilvoll. Man kann schwimmen, Tennis spielen, reiten, gut essen – oder einfach nur faulenzen. Nach der Siesta könnte man sich aufraffen zu einer kleinen Wanderung auf die arabische Burg Castell d'Alaró, die eine herrliche Aussicht bietet. Das dauert rund drei Stunden. Auf jeden Fall ist man rechtzeitig zum Sherry und jenem Konzert zurück, das allabendlich die Grillen in dieser biblischen Einöde aufführen.

Cheerful isolation

A quiet village in cheerful isolation. That's how one imagines country life on Mallorca. A handful of quarry-stone houses with a church surrounded by a huge garden full of grapevines, lemon and apple orchards, olive and almond trees. There is a scent of flowers and wild herbs. That is important, because some of the plants are harvested here for the Mallorcan herb liqueur "Hierbas" which is drunk all over the Balearic Islands. You can try it in the village bar: sweet for the ladies, sharp for the men. After the aperitif you go to the "L'Hermitage", a former finca (estate) which is under a preservation order, where exhausted nomadic monks were once given food and lodging. Today's guests are spoiled in an extremely stylish way. You can go swimming, play tennis, ride horses, have fantastic meals – or simply laze about. After the siesta you could decide to go for a hike to the Arabian castle Castell d'Alaró (fantastic view). It takes about three hours. And you get back in time for a sherry and the concert that the crickets perform every evening in this splendid isolation.

Binissalem | Dorf an der Weinstrasse

Es Foro de Mallorca
Di.-So. 10-13.30 Uhr, 14.30-19 Uhr

23 Mallorca hat inzwischen mehrere Weinstraßen. Die älteste führt von Santa Maria über Consell nach Binissalem. Dieses ruhige, in den letzten Jahren hübsch herausgeputzte Dorf feiert in der letzten Septemberwoche nach der Weinlese seine festa des vermar, sein Weinfest; richtig mit Weinkönigin und Weinseligkeit und mit einem köstlichen Essen für alle Einheimischen und Fremden an langen Tischen in engen Gassen. Auf den Tisch kommt die fideuà, ein Kaninchen-Nudeltopf, und natürlich krügeweise Heuriger. Den Winzern hat Binissalem ein Denkmal gesetzt, direkt an der alten Pfarrkirche L'Asumpció aus dem 13. Jahrhundert. Schräg gegenüber versteckt sich ein zauberhafter, blumengeschmückter Innenhof, um den herum sich die Zimmer des kleinen Dorfhotels "Scott's" befinden. Der Name Binissalem verrät die arabische Gründung.
Im 3 km entfernten "Es Foro de Mallorca" gibt es ein Wachsfigurenkabinett. Dort stehen viele herum, die mal was zu sagen hatten auf Mallorca: Araber, Römer, Vandalen, Christen, natürlich die balearischen Steinschleuderer, der Maler Joan Miró und der Denker Ramón Llull. Auch die spanische Königsfamilie blickt – allerdings nicht ganz vollzählig –, stumm und würdig drein.

Village on the Wine Road

In the meantime, Mallorca has several Wine Roads. The oldest leads from Santa Maria via Consell to Binissalem. This quiet village, which has been nicely smartened up in the past years, celebrates its Festa des Vermar, its wine festival, on the last week in September with a Wine Queen and wine atmosphere, and with delicious food for all local people and strangers on long tables in narrow alleys. Fidluà, a rabbit stew, is served, and of course, jugs of local wine. The wine-growers of Binissalem have been given a monument next to the old parish church L'Asumpció from the 13th century. Diagonally opposite is hidden a delightful inner courtyard decorated with flowers, around which are the rooms of the small village hotel "Scott's". The name Binissalem reveals the Arabian founding. In "Es Foro de Mallorca", 3 km away, there is a waxworks museum. Many figures stand around who once had something to say on Mallorca: Arabs, Romans, Vandals, Christians, of course the Balearic catapult throwers, the artist Joan Miró and the philosopher Ramón Llull. Even the Spansih Royal Family is present – not quite complete, but silent and dignified.

Inca | Küche im Keller

24 Schuld waren die Römer und die Araber. Sie brachten den Wein mit nach Mallorca. Es entstanden Weinberge – und die `cellers´, die typischen Weinkeller. Dann kamen die Christen, und irgendwann einmal kam die Reblaus. Und die hatte letztendlich an allem Schuld. Sie fraß die Rebstöcke kurz und klein, brachte den Weinbau zum Erliegen. Die Weinkeller jedoch blieben bestehen. Man stellte Stühle und Tische zwischen die Fässer und tischte auf. Zunächst nur Kleinigkeiten, dann aber wurden die `cellers´ zu einer typischen mallorquinischen Einrichtung, in der die deftige Bauernküche der Insel serviert wurde. Das ist bis heute so geblieben. Und auch der Weinbau ist wieder in Schwung gekommen, so dass niemand in den "cellers" verdursten muss. Im Zentrum laden Fußgängerzonen, hübsche Plätze, lebhafte Einkaufsstraßen und der Wochenmarkt am Donnerstag zum Verweilen ein. Berühmt ist Inca für ihre Lederproduktion. An der Durchgangsstraße Palma-Alcúdia liegen die Schau- und Verkaufsräume von fast einem halben Dutzend Firmen. Vor allem Schuhe lohnen einen Besuch; sie sind hier sehr viel preiswerter als daheim.

Cuisine in the cellar

The Romans and the Arabs were to blame. They introduced wine to Mallorca. Vineyards were made – along with the "cellers", the typical wine cellars. Then the Christians came, and at some time or other a little guest that goes by the Latin name of phylloscera. And that was finally to blame for everything. It ate away the vines till they were bare and that was the end of wine-growing. But the wine-cellars remained – and how! Chairs and tables were put between the barrels and guests were served. At first just snacks, but then the "cellers" became a typically Mallorcan establishment where food from the island was served. And that's what it's still like today. And wine-growing has been revived so that no one has to die of thirst in the "cellers". In the centre pedestrian zones, pretty squares, lively shopping streets and on Thursdays the weekly market invite one to stay a while. Inca is famous for its leather production. Almost half a dozen salesrooms are situated on the through road Palma-Alcúdia. Shoes, above all, are more reasonable in price than at home.

Selva | Berge und Oliven

25 Mallorca ist eigentlich eine Insel der Bauern. Sogar die Berghänge wurden landwirtschaftlich genutzt. Das machten schon die Araber und vor ihnen die Römer, die höchstwahrscheinlich den Olivenbaum mitbrachten. Die Mauren haben diese Kultur perfektioniert. Selbst auf kargstem Felsboden und in Steillagen legten sie Oliventerrassen an. Noch heute stehen zwischen Fornalutx und Inca Hunderttausende von Ölbäumen, von denen einige etliche hundert Jahre alt sind. Das Öl aus dieser Region gilt als das beste der Balearen. Nach dem ersten Tourismus-Boom in den 1960er-Jahren vernachlässigte man die Olivenbäume und die Ölgewinnung; die tafones (Ölmühlen) standen still. Später jedoch besann man sich im Raum Sóller, Caimari und Selva auf die alte Tradition und verarbeitete wieder Oliven zu Speiseöl. Heute wetteifern Sóller und Caimari mit alljährlichen Oliven-Messen im Winter um die Gunst ihrer Besucher. Da kann jeder eingelegte grüne und schwarze Oliven verkosten, kaltgepresstes Olivenöl auf mallorquinischem Brot probieren und zuschauen, wie eine tafona funktioniert. Im Frühjahr jedoch blüht Selva im wahrsten Sinne des Wortes auf: Millionen Mandelbaumblüten überziehen dann die Täler und Berghänge rundherum mit einem weiß-rosa Schleier.

Mountains and olives

Mallorca was originally an island of farmers. Even the mountain slopes were used for agriculture. The Arabs did that, and the Romans before them, who probably brought the olive tree with them. The Moors perfected this culture. They built olive terraces even on barren rocky ground and on steep escarpments. Between Fornalutx and Inca you can still see hundreds of thousands of olive trees, many of which are hundreds of years old. The oil from this region is considered to be the best on the Balearic Islands. After the first tourist boom in the 1960s the olive trees and oil production were neglected: the "tafones" (oil mills) stood still. Later, however, in the area around Sóller, Caimari and Selva, the old tradition was revived and olive oil was once again produced. Today Sóller and Caimari compete with each other every winter with olive fairs. Visitors can try the pickled green and black olives, taste the cold-pressed olive oil on Mallorcan bread and watch how a "tafona" works. In spring, however, Selva really blossoms: millions of almond blossoms then cover the valleys and mountain slopes with a white-pink veil.

Fornalutx | Am Fuße der Berge

26 Wie ein beschützender Pate erhebt sich der Puig Major, mit 1443 Meter der höchste Berg Mallorcas, über Fornalutx. Das Gebirgsdorf hat sich in ein Tal der Farben und Düfte gebettet. An den Palmen hängen Dattelstauden, aus dem Immergrün der Orangenhaine blinken die goldfarbenen Früchte wie Sterne. Ein Garten Eden, durch den das betörende Aroma von Zitronen und wildem Majoran zieht. Diese Kulisse rahmt einen Ort, der zweimal zum schönsten Dorf Spaniens gekürt wurde. Solche Auszeichnungen sind nicht immer ein Segen. Im Sommer wird in Fornalutx mehr Deutsch und Englisch gesprochen als Mallorquin; die Einwohnerzahl verdoppelt sich von 600 auf 1200. Dennoch kann man kaum von Trubel sprechen; die Gäste von Fornalutx wissen, was sie diesem Ort und seinem Ambiente schuldig sind. Fornalutx, von Arabern gegründet, hat einige Wurzeln auch jenseits des Meeres. Als im Mittelalter die Pest die meisten Einwohner dahinraffte, wurden Einwanderer aus Italien geholt.
Wer möchte, probiert in einer der Cafeterías frischgepressten Orangensaft und schlendert dann in die Straße `Carrer de Sa Font': an den Häusern mit den Nummern 7 und 8 entdeckt man an den überkragenden Dachschindeln hübsche Malereien.

At the foot of the mountains

The Puig Major, Mallorca's highest mountain at 1,443 metres, rises over Fornalutx like a protective godfather. The mountain village is embedded in a valley full of colours and scents. Bunches of dates hang from the palm trees and the golden oranges shine like stars from the evergreen orange groves. A Garden of Eden with the captivating aroma of lemons and wild marjoram. This scenery surrounds a village which has twice been chosen as the most beautiful village in Spain. Such honours aren't always a blessing. In summer more German and English is spoken than Mallorcan: the population doubles from 600 to 1,200. And yet one cannot speak of hustle and bustle; the guests in Fornalutx know what they owe to this village and its ambience. Fornalutx, which was founded by Arabs, also has some of its roots beyond the sea. When most of its inhabitants died of the plague in the Middle Ages, immigrants from Italy were fetched. Tip: you really must try the freshly pressed orange juice in one of the Cafeterías, and look for the street Carrer de Sa Font: look up at the houses Nr. 7 and 8 and admire the paintings.

Sa Calobra | Die Straße nach nirgendwo

27 Wie eine Schlange windet sich die Straße durch das Gebirge. In zahllosen Kurven und Serpentinen überwindet sie 800 Höhenmeter. Warum? Weil es 1932 ihr Baumeister Chefingenieur Parietti sinnvoll fand, mit 15 Kilometer Straße gerade mal vier Kilometer voranzukommen. Ziel war das Meer, eine Bucht und das Nest Sa Calobra, ein idyllisches Nichts. Dort lebten seit Jahrhunderten sechs Familien, die so von der Zivilisation abgeschnitten waren, dass sie nicht einmal Spanisch, sondern nur Mallorquin sprachen. Früher führte nur ein Fußpfad durch die Berge ins Inselinnere. Heute wird Sa Calobra von unzähligen Ausflugsbussen angefahren. Eine breite Uferpromenade führt an einem Hotel, an Restaurants und Souvenirläden vorbei und verjüngt sich schließlich zu zwei engen Fußgänger-Tunnel. An deren Ende warten grandiose Anblicke: das breite Kiesbett-Tal des Torrent de Pareis und seine Mündung zum blauen Meer, gerahmt von kolossalen, himmelhohen Felswänden.

Für trainierte Wanderer startet ab Escorca eine mehr als sechsstündige, schwere Kletterpartie hinab durch den zweitgrößten Canyon Europas. Nur in trockenen Monaten sollte man diese nicht ungefährliche Tour durch enge Steilwände und fantastische Höhlen wagen.

The road to nowhere

The road winds through the mountains like a snake. It surmounts 800 metres in numerous hairpin bends. Why? Because in 1932 its builder, chief engineer Parietti, considered it sensible to cover a distance of four kilometres with 15 km of road. The destination was the sea, a bay and the hamlet Sa Calobra, an idyllic nothing. For centuries six families lived there, and they were so cut off from civilization that they didn't even speak Spanish, but only Mallorcan. Today Sa Calobra is visited by countless excursion buses, whose journey ends on a huge car-park. A wide shore promenade leads past a hotel, restaurants and souvenir shops and finally changes to two narrow pedestrian tunnels. At their end there are magnificent views: the wide pebble-bed valley of the Torrent de Pareis and its mouth at the blue sea, framed by colossal sky-high cliffs. For practised hikers from Escorca starts a more than six-hour-long, difficult climb down through the second-largest canyon in Europe. One should only risk this tour, which is not without danger, through narrow rock walls and fantastic caves in dry months.

Kloster Lluc | Ein großes Kloster für die kleine Madonna

28 Die Legende von der Moreneta ist wie alle Legenden eine hübsche Geschichte. Es war einmal ein maurischer Hirtenjunge, der eines Tages eine Madonnenfigur fand. Ihre Schönheit strahlte so viel Güte und Gnade aus, dass der kleine Maure nur noch einen Wunsch hatte: der Moreneta eine ihr gebührende Kapelle zu bauen. Das war, so geht die Kunde, der Anfang der Abtei Lluc, des bedeutendsten Klosters und Wallfahrtsorts Mallorcas. Mittlerweile ist er auch ein Anziehungspunkt für Tagestouristen, denn Kloster Lluc beherbergt ein sehenswertes Museum, ausgedehnte Picknickplätze unter Eichen sowie einige Restaurants, in denen Spezialitäten wie tumbet (Gemüsetopf) oder cabrit (Zickleinbraten) serviert werden. Wer vor dem Ansturm der Tagesgäste fliehen und zu ausgedehnten Wanderungen aufbrechen möchte, wer die klösterliche Ruhe abends und morgens sucht, kann sich in den ehemaligen Mönchszellen einquartieren; sie sind preiswert, alles andere als karg und sogar zentralbeheizt. Man wohnt Wand an Wand mit den Knaben einer Singschule, die seit dem 16. Jh. in Lluc untergebracht ist. Die blavets im weißblauen Gewand singen jeden Morgen um 11.15 Uhr Choräle zur Messe.

The monastery and the barman

The legend of the Moreneta is, like all legends, a nice story. There was once a Moorish shepherd boy who one day found a statue of the Madonna. Its beauty radiated so much goodness and grace that the little Moor had only one wish: to build a fitting chapel for the Moreneta. That is said to be the beginning of Lluc Abbey, the most important monastery and place of pilgrimage on Mallorca. In the meantime it has also become an attraction for day trippers, because Lluc Monastery not only has several souvenir shops, but also an interesting museum, extensive picnic areas beneath oak trees as well as some restaurants where specialities like tumbet, a vegetable stew, or cabrit, roast kid, are served. Those wanting to flee from the onslaught of the day-trippers and set off on long walks, those seeking monastic peace in the mornings and evenings, can stay in the former monks'cells: they are good value; far from being poor and even have central heating. One lives wall-to-wall with the boys of a choir school, which has been in Lluc since the 16th C. The blavets in their blue-white gowns sing chorales for mass every mornig at 11.15 am.

Pollença | Archaische Feste

29 Die Römer waren vor ungefähr 2000 Jahren schon mal dort. Sie hinterließen eine kleine Brücke. Der dazugehörige Ort kam erst wesentlich später. Er entstand aus einem Versteck, denn die Bewohner des nahen Ortes Alcúdia, einer arabischen Gründung, waren es leid, ständig von Piraten überfallen zu werden. Sie gründeten im 14. Jh. in der Nähe der Römerbrücke eine kleine Stadt, die sie Pollentia nannten, nach einer Römersiedlung, die sich einst bei Alcúdia befand. Der Sieg der christlichen Pollenciner über türkische Piraten im Jahr 1550 feiert Jahr für Jahr am 2. August fröhliche Auferstehung: 500 pluderbehoste Piraten prallen mit mörderischem Gebrüll auf 500 Christen in weißen Nachthemden (der Angriff geschah nachts); Höhepunkt und Abschluss des Patronatsfestes. Ebenfalls im Hochsommer erscheinen hochkarätige Interpreten zum Internationalen Musikfestival im luftigen Klosterhof Santo Domingo. 365 Stufen (für jeden Tage des Jahres eine) führten ursprünglich auf den Kalvarienberg; jüngst kamen noch einige dazu, weil man den Blick zur Kapelle weiten wollte. Von dort tragen am Karfreitag stumme Büßer eine dunkelhäutige Christusfigur in einer eindrucksvollen Prozession zur Pfarrkirche hinab, in der an Himmelfahrt die Aguiles (Adlermädchen) tanzen. Auf ihren Brusttüchern prangen uralte, sehr wertvolle Schmuckstücke, die pollencinische Bürgerinnen für dieses Fest aus der Schatulle geholt und ausgeliehen haben.

Archaic festival

The Romans were already there. About 2,000 years ago. They left a small bridge. The town belonging to it only came much later. It was created from a hiding-place, because the inhabitants of the nearby town Alcúdia, an Arab foundation, were sick of continually being attacked by pirates. In the 14th C they founded a little town near the Roman bridge and named it Pollentia, after a Roman settlement, which was once situated near Alcúdia. The victory of the Christian Pollentians over Turkish pirates in 1550 is celebrated once again every year on 2 August: 500 pirates in pantaloons collide with murderous roars with 500 Christians in white nightdresses (the attack took place at night): the highlight and conclusion of the patronate festival. Afterwards there come: top-class interpreters appear at the International Music Festival in the airy monastery courtyard Santo Domingo (July/Aug.). 365 steps (one for each day of the year) originally led to Mount Calvary. Recently several have been added in order to widen the view onto the chapel. On Good Friday silent penitents carry a dark-skinned figure of Christ down in an impressive procession to the parish church, where on Ascension Day the Aguiles (eagle girls) dance.

Cala Sant Vicenç | Der Zauberberg und die Zauberbucht

30 Wie ein Camäleon ändert er seine Farbe: morgens ragt seine Silhouette unnahbar schwarz wie eine Barriere aus dem Meer, mittags döst er in Ockertönen vor sich hin, abends färbt ihn die untergehende Sonne feuerrot, bevor er im letzten Widerschein der Sonne lilablau in der Dämmerung versinkt. Er ist wahrlich ein Zauberberg, der "Cavall Bernat", Wahrzeichen von Cala Sant Vicenç. Und auch die Badebuchten überraschen mit extrem unterschiedlichen Stimmungen: bei Landwind schwappt das Meer träge wie ein See, kristallklar türkis bis kobaltblau ist sein Wasser – ideal für Schwimmer und Taucher, die hier eine buntschillernde Unterwasserwelt bestaunen können. Bei stürmischem Nordwind bäumen sich meterhohe Wellen auf, schäumt weiße Gischt über Strand und Fels, verwandelt sich die Mittelmeerküste in ein Stück wilde Bretagne. Hier gibt es viel Ruhe, kleine Familienbuchten, ein paar reizvolle Wanderwege und einige Restaurants vor einer grandiosen Naturkulisse.

The magic mountain and magic bay

It changes its colour like a chameleon: in the morning its silhouette towers up unapproachably black like a barrier out of the sea, at midday it dozes in shades of ochre, in the evening the sinking sun colours it a fiery-red before in the last reflection of the sun it sinks lilac-blue in the dusk. It truly is a magic mountain, the "Cavall Bernat", symbol of Cala Sant Vicenç. And the bathing coves are surprising too with their extremely different atmospheres: with offshore winds the sea splashes lazily like a lake, its water is crystal-clear turquoise to colbalt blue – ideal for swimmers and divers who can admire a colourful underwater world here. When there is a stormy north wind metre-high waves tower up, white spray foams over the beach and rocks, and the Mediterranean coast transforms itself into a part of wild Brittany. Here one can find peace and quiet, little family coves, a few charming trails and some good restaurants in front of an exceptionally magnificent nature backcloth.

Formentor | Traumhaftes Ende

31 Die hochdramatische Landschaft dieser Halbinsel im äußersten Norden Mallorcas ist ein absolutes "Muss". Bis zu 400 Meter tief stürzen die steilen Klippen ins Meer. Der Blick hinab vom "Mirador" auf der ersten Passhöhe der Straße von Port de Pollenca erzeugt Gänsehaut. Wild schäumt das Meer tief unten – auch um den Colomer (das Wort leitet sich von colóm = Taube ab), einen unbewohnten Felsklotz, auf dem Möwen und wilde Tauben nisten. Den Besitzern des legendären Hotels "Formentor" gehört die ganze Halbinsel, die außer ein paar Luxusvillen prominenter Künstler und Staatsmänner keine weitere Bebauung aufweist. Natur pur also, ausgedehnte Pinienwälder und windzerzauste Zwergpalmen, gigantische Felsformationen und bilderbuchschöne Strände. Belebt ist die Cala Pi de la Posada unterhalb des Hotels, in dessen blumigen Terrassengarten ein Kaffeepäuschen zu empfehlen ist. Bei km 12 in Richtung Cap Formentor führt ein ziemlich steiler Weg hinab zur Cala Figuera. Nach einem etwa 20-minütigen Fußmarsch erreicht man die naturbelassene, mit rund geschliffenen Kieselsteinen übersäte Sandbucht. Sie werden zwar nicht ganz mit sich allein sein, aber immerhin mit nur wenigen Gleichgesinnten.

Fantastic end

The dramatic landscape of this peninsula in the extreme north of Mallorca is an absolute "must". The steep cliffs drop up to 400 m into the sea. The view down from the "Mirador" on the first pass altitude of the road from Port de Pollença gives you goose pimples. The sea foams deep below also around the Colomer (the word derives from colóm = dove), an uninhabited rock on which seagulls and doves nest. Just nature, extensive pine forests and wind-blown dwarf palms, gigantic rock formations and beaches like out of a picture-book. Very lively, and above all on Sundays overcrowed is the Cala Ti de la Posada below the hotel, where a coffee break in its flowery terrace garden is to be recommended. At km 12 in the direction of Cap Formentor a rather steep path leads down to Cala Figuera. After a 20-minute walk from here you reach the natural Cala Figuera. You won't be quite alone with yourself, sun, sand and sea, but there will only be a few like-minded.

Alcúdia | Die Rivalin von Palma

32 Alcúdia ist so etwas wie Mallorcas gute Stube. Eine intakte mittelalterliche Stadtmauer umschließt den Ort, den man durch das Stadttor Puerta de Sant Sebastiá betritt. Die alten engen Gassen wichen Fußgängerzonen, das Städtchen wurde vorbildlich saniert. Die Römer siedelten als erste hier. Sie bauten die Stadt Pollentia auf, die um 450 n. Chr. verfiel. Fast 500 Jahre tat sich dann nichts. Schließlich kamen die Araber und bauten auf einem nahegelegenen Hügel mit den Steinen des verfallenen Pollentia eine neue Stadt auf. Sie wurde die Residenz Mallorcas. Diese Würde ging erst später auf Palma über, was eine Rivalität zwischen den Städten auslöste, die bis heute anhält.
Zu den großen Sehenswürdigkeiten der Stadt zählen neben der gotischen Pfarrkirche Sant Jaume das alte römische Theater sowie das Ruinenfeld von Pollentia an der Straße nach Port Alcúdia. Port Alcúdia ist in den Sommermonaten ein turbulenter Ferienort mit großen Hotels und einem ausgeprägten Nachtleben. In Alcúdia leben und arbeiten viele "foresters", Zugereiste von der iberischen Halbinsel. Die von Andalusiern geführten Tapa-Bars lohnen einen Besuch.

Palma's rival

Alcúdia is the showpiece of Mallorca. An intact medieval wall surrounds the town which you enter through the town gate Puerta de Sant Sebastiá. The old, narrow streets make room for pedestrian zones, the little town has been redeveloped in an exemplary way. The Romans first settled here. They built the town of Pollentia, which was destroyed in about 450 AD. For nearly 500 years almost nothing happened. Then the Arabs came and built a new town on a nearby hill ('Arabian: alkudia) with the stones of the destroyed Pollentia. It became Mallorca's capital. This honour was later transferred to Palma which sparked off a rivalry between the two towns which still exists today. The sights of the town include the Gothic parish church, Sant Jaume, the old Roman theatre and the ruins of Pollentia on the road to Port Alcúdia. Port Alcúdia is a turbulent holiday resort in the summer months with large hotels and a distinctive night life.

Badia d'Alcúdia | Der Strand der Surfer

33 Eigentlich müßte man im selben Atemzug mit der größten Bucht Mallorcas auch die Badía de Pollenca nennen. Die Doppelbucht misst fast 50 Kilometer vorwiegend sandige Küste. Wenn eine leichte Brise die Wellen aufschäumt, ist das beste Wetter für die Windsurfer. Es ist ein malerisches Bild, wenn die bunten Segel über das blaue, blinkende Wasser flitzen. Die Doppelbucht ist neben den Stränden an der Südküste (bei Sa Rápita) das beste Surfrevier der Insel. Nicht von ungefähr ist in Port de Pollenca seit über 30 Jahren die größte Segel- und Surfschule des Mittelmeerraumes ("Sail & Surf", deutsche Leitung) zuhause. Die Badeorte an der Badía d'Alcúdia bieten für junge Leute auch das entsprechende Nightlife. Das heißt: Es geht drunter und drüber. Can Picafort, das nicht unbedingt durch seine architektonische Schönheit besticht, wird eigentlich erst nach Sonnenuntergang wach. Und erst recht Port d'Alcúdia. In dem 35 000-Betten-Zentrum tobt nachts der Bär. Strandschlaf vorausgesetzt, denn vor 1 Uhr tut sich nichts. Danach geht Sommernacht für Sommernacht die Post ab ... Der Strandabschnitt Platja de Muro erhielt eine Reihe neuer, familienfreundlicher Hotels. Viel Kinderanimation rund um die Uhr entlasten gestresste Eltern, die sich am weißen Dünensand dem süßen Nichtstun hingeben können.

The surfers' beach

In the same breath one really ought to mention the Badía de Pollença with the largest bay on Mallorca. The twin bay measures almost 50 km mainly sandy coastline. When a light breeze makes the waves foam it's the best weather for the windsurfers. It's a picturesque scene when the colourful sails shoot across the blue sparkling water. Next to the beaches on the south coast (near Sa Rápita) the twin bay is the best place for surfing on the island. It is no accident that for 30 years the largest sailing and surfing school in the Meditteranean is at home in Port de Pollença ("Sail & Surf", under German direction). The seaside resorts on the Badía d'Alcúdia also offer plenty of night life. That means it's very turbulent. Can Picafort, which doesn't really stand out for its architectural beauty, only really wakes up after sunset. And even more so Port d'Acúdia. In the 35,000-bed centre the nights are wild. Provided you've had a sleep on the beach, that is, because there's nothing going on before 1am. Then, one summer night after the other all hell's let loose...

Artà | Eine feste Burg

34 Egal, aus welcher Richtung: Artà kann sich sehen lassen. Eine trutzige Zitadelle krönt das Landstädtchen im Nordosten. Und wie eine weitere feste Burg erhebt sich aus ihr die Wallfahrtskirche Sant Salvador – auch wieder eine arabische Bastion ("artan" = arabisch Garten), sogar die führende von 12 Distrikten. Doch Artàs Geschichte ist noch viel älter, wie talayotische Funde aus der Bronzezeit dokumentieren. Hinter dem stillgelegten Bahnhof versteckt sich in einem Eichenhain ´Ses Paisses´, eine der gepflegtesten Talayot-Siedlungen der Insel. Hier lebten vor dreitausend Jahren Menschen in 60 Räumen rund um den Talayot, den Wacht- und Verteidigungsturm und Wohnsitz der Oberhäupter. Nur die Siedlung von Capicorb Vell im Inselsüden ist noch vergleichbar gut erhalten.

Auch Capdepera, 8 km weiter östlich, wird von einer eindrucksvollen Burganlage gekrönt. Von dort geht der Blick bis zur Nachbarinsel Menorca und weit über die Halbinsel Ferrutx mit ihren verkarsteten Bergen und vielen versteckten Sandbuchten. Und zu den weißen Hotelbauten von Cala Rajada, die nicht ahnen lassen, dass sich hinter ihnen mehrere schöne Sandstrände und ein hübscher Hafen verbergen.

Ses Paisses
April-Sept.
Mo.-Sa. 9.30-13 Uhr, 16-19.30 Uhr

Castell de Capdepera
Sommer:
tgl. 9-20 Uhr,
Winter:
tgl. 9-17 Uhr

A strong castle

No matter from which direction: Artà can show itself. A formidable citadel crowns the little country town in the north-east. And like another strong castle, the pilgrimage church Sant Salvador rises above it – also an Arabian bastion ("Artan" = Arabian garden), in fact the leading one of 12 districts. But Artàs'-history is much older, as Talayotic finds from the Bronze Age demonstrate. Behind the closed railway station in an oak grove Ses Paisses is hidden one of the best-kept Talayot settlements of the island. 30 centuries ago people lived here around the Talayot, the watch- and defence-tower and residence of the chieftains. Only the settlement in the south of the island is equally well preserved. Capdepera, 8 km further east, is also crowned by an impressive castle. From its battlements the view stretches as far as the neighbouring island Menorca and far across the peninsula Farrutx with its karstified mountains and many hidden sandy bays. And to the white hotel buildings of Cala Rajada, which give no idea that behind them several beautiful sandy bays and one of the prettiest island harbours are hidden.

Coves del Drac | Showtime unter Tage

35 Die Drachenhöhle gehört zu den größten Attraktionen Mallorcas. Das war sie schon im Altertum. Damals versteckten sich die Mallorquiner zwischen den Tropfsteinsäulen vor anrückenden Feinden. Doch erst 1896 wurde die große Höhle erforscht. Diesen Verdienst erwarb sich der Franzose Edouard Marte. Er entdeckte dabei auch den weltgrößten unterirdischen See, der nach ihm benannt wurde. Der Llac Martel ist 177 Meter lang, 40 Meter breit und bis zu neun Meter tief. Sein Wasser ist glasklar. Die Führung (etwa 90 Minuten) durch die fantastisch ausgeleuchtete Höhle gehört zu den Höhepunkten eines Mallorca-Urlaubs. Vor dem See nehmen die Besucher auf Holztribünen Platz. Dann erklingt klassische Musik: Zwei beleuchtete Boote gleiten über das Wasser, Musikstudenten intonieren schluchzende Klassik. Ein kitschigschönes Touristenspektakel.

Szenenwechsel: Gleich am Ortseingang von Portocristo versuchen die 'Coves d'es Hams' den Drachenhöhlen Konkurrenz zu machen – untertage, mit einer virtuellen Jules Verne-Show. Natürlicher präsentiert sich Mallorcas Unterwelt in den Höhlen von Artà mit ihrem rauchgeschwärzten, schlundartigen Eingang über dem Meer und die kleinen aber feinen Coves de Campanet mit zum Teil spaghettidünnen Stalagmiten.

Coves del Drac
Führungen Sommer: 10-17 Uhr (zu jeder vollen Stunde)
Führungen Winter: 10.45, 12, 14 und 15.30 Uhr

Coves d'Artà
Sommer: tgl. 10-18.30 Uhr, Winter: tgl. 10-17 Uhr

Coves d'es Hams
Sommer: tgl. 10-17.30 Uhr, Winter: tgl. 10.30-16.30 Uhr

Coves de Campanet
tgl. 10-17 Uhr

Showtime beneath the ground

The dragon's cave is one of the main attractions on Mallorca. This was already the case in antiquity, when the Mallorcans hid from the approaching enemy between the stalactites and stalagmites. But the large cave was only explored in 1896 by a foreigner: the Frenchman Edouard Martel also discovered the largest underground lake in the world, which was named after him. The Llac Martel is 177 metres long, 40 metres wide and up to 9 metres deep. Its water is crystal clear. The tour through the fantastically illuminated cave lasts about 90 minutes and is one of the highlights of a holiday on Mallorca. The visitors sit on wooden benches in front of the lake. Then classical music is played, which gradually comes nearer: two illuminated boats glide over the water, music students play sobbing classical music. A kitschig-fine tourist spectacle. Chance of scene: directly at the start of Portocristo the "Coves d'es Hams" try to compete against the dragon's cave – underground, with a virtual Jules Verne Show. Of course Mallorca's underworld presents itself in the caves of Artà with smoke-blakkened, gaping entrance above the sea and the small but fine Coves de Campanet with partly spaghetti-thin stalagmites.

Costa de Llevant | Paradies nach dem Sündenfall

36 Unzählige kleine und kleinste calas gliedern die Ostküste wie ein Sägeblatt. Sattgrüne Pinien, goldgelber Sand, weißgetünchte Häuser und das türkisblaue Meer – Mallorcas heiterste Seite könnte die schönste sein, wären da nicht in den Hochsommermonaten viel zu viele Urlauber in viel zu vielen Hotels und viel zu viele Jachten, die in den fjordähnlichen Buchten ankern. Dennoch, wer sucht, der findet seine kleine Bucht ohne Rummel. Die Suche ist ein wenig mühsam, weil es keine verbindende Küstenstraße gibt. So muss man von der langen Landstraße über die Hügel der Serra de Llevant immer wieder auf Stichstraßen zu den einzelnen calas fahren. Die lieblichsten liegen zwischen Portocolom und der Küste um Santanyí: die nur zu Fuß erreichbare winzige und total unbebaute Cala Brafi, die ebenfalls unbebaute Cala Arsenau, die unter Naturschutz gestellte malerische Doppelbucht Cala Mondragó, die allerdings im Sommer stark besucht wird, die kleine hotelgesäumte Familienbucht von Santanyí, die vor allem von jungen Leuten geliebte Cala Llombarts und die nur mit Fußmärschen erreichbaren, versteckten Naturbuchten von s'Amúnia und sa Comuna. Die tief eingeschnittene Cala Figuera hat zwar gar keinen Sandstrand, ist jedoch einer der idyllischsten Fischerhäfen der Insel.

Paradise after the fall from grace

Countless small and tiny calas line along the east coast like a saw blade. Bright green pine trees, golden sands, whitewashed houses and the turquoise sea – Mallorca's cheeriest side could also be the most beautiful, if it weren't for far too many tourists and far too many yachts. However, seek and you shall find your own little bay without bustle. The search isn't exactly easy because there is no connecting coastal road. And so one has to leave the long road over the hills of the Serra de Llevant again and again to drive along cul-de-sacs to the individual calas. The most charming lie between Portocolom and the coast around Santayí: the tiny and completely undeveloped Cala Brafi which can only be reached on foot, the protected picturesque twin bay Cala Mondragó, which is however overcrowded in summer, the little hotel-lined family bay of Santanyí, the Cala Llombarts, particularly popular with young people, and the hidden natural bay of s'Amúnia. The deeply indented Cala Figuera has no sandy beach, but is one of the most idyllic fishing harbours.

Es Trenc | Der Dünenstrand

37 Es Trenc dürfte der bekannteste Strand Mallorcas sein. Und er ist auch einer der schönsten: drei Kilometer unverbautes Meeresufer mit kiefernbestandenen Dünen. Berühmt wurde Es Trenc nicht nur durch seinen Nacktbadeabschnitt, sondern durch eine Protestwelle, die letztendlich den Strand rettete. Bei Ses Covetes sollte ein gigantisches Hotel errichtet werden. Mallorquinische Umweltschützer gründeten die Bewegung "Salvem Es Trenc" – rettet Es Trenc. Sie erinnerten die Verantwortlichen nachdrücklich an den weiten Strand von s'Arenal, der heute als der verbauteste Schandfleck im gesamten Mittelmeerraum gilt. Einst war auch s'Arenal ein Stück unverfälschte Natur – wie Es Trenc. Das Hotelvorhaben wurde gestoppt.

Im Hafen von Colónia de Sant Jordi startet sommers täglich um 9 Uhr ein Ausflugsdampfer zu einer sehr reizvollen Tagesfahrt nach Cabrera, dem von überall sichtbaren naturgeschützten, unbewohnten Archipel vor der Südküste.

In Ses Salines freut sich ein sympathischer Wirt in seiner urigen Fischerkneipe an der Kirche auf ihren Besuch. Er holt seinen Hummer und anderes Meeresgetier aus den kristallklaren Wassern Cabreras und bereitet eine auf der Insel einmalige Köstlichkeit zu: den arròs de notari, einen Reistopf mit Hummer.

The dune beach

Es Trenc might be the best-known beach on Mallorca. And it is also one of the most beautiful: three kilometres of undeveloped seashore with pine-covered dunes. Es Trenc became famous not only because of its nudist beach but also because of a wave of protest which finally rescued the beach. Near Ses Covetes a gigantic hotel was going to be built. Mallorcan environmentalists founded the movement "Salvem Es Trenc" – rescue Es Trenc. They expressly reminded those responsible of the wide beach of s'Arenal, which is nowadays considered to be the worst built-up blot of the whole Mediterranean. Once s'Arenal was also a piece of untouched nature – like El Trenc. The hotel development project was stopped. In the harbour of Colónia de Sant Jordi, an excursion steamer sets off on a very charming day trip to Cabrera, the uninhabited archipelago of the south coast, protected by law and visible from everywhere. In Ses Salines a friendly landlord is pleased by a visit to his cosy fish restaurant near the church. He gets his lobsters and fresh fish from the crystal clear waters of Cabrera.

Sant Joan | Leben nach Gutsherrenart

Landgut Els Calderés
Sommer:
tgl. 10-18 Uhr,
Winter:
tgl. 10-17 Uhr

38 Hat nicht soeben der Gutsherr in seinem Adelszimmer über Getreidepreise debattiert? Und hat die Dame des Hauses nicht vor fünf Minuten die gedeckte Tafel gemustert und schnell noch ein fehlendes Weinglas hinzugestellt? Unglaublich, wie selbstverständlich alle Dinge an ihrem Platz stehen, in den Salons, auf den Terrassen, in den Handwerksstuben und Ställen des Landgutes Els Calderés bei Sant Joan. Erst vor ein paar Jahren verließen die adligen Besitzer ihren feudalen Herrensitz und zogen in ihren Stadtpalast nach Palma. Sie beließen alles so, wie es seit Jahrhunderten üblich war. So erhält der Besucher einen unverfälschten Eindruck vom Leben auf einem Landgut. Heute gibt es noch 500 autonome Güter auf der Insel. Landwirtschaftlich nicht mehr rentabel, denkt der Landadel um und verwandelt die zum Teil imposanten Güter in Pensionen, Hotels, Restaurants und Nachtclubs. Oder eben in ein Museum wie Els Calderés, von dessen Vergangenheit als Weingut noch der prächtige Weinkeller zeugt und als Getreidegut die riesige Kornkammer im Obergeschoss. An den weißgekalkten Wänden leuchten rote Tomatenzöpfe, die die Insulaner bis heute für ihr geliebtes "pa amb oli" (Tomaten-Brot mit Olivenöl) verwenden.

Living like the lord of the manor

Hasn't the lord of the manor just been discussing the corn prices in his aristocratic room? And didn't the lady of the house take a look at the set table five minutes ago and quickly added a missing wine glass? It's unbelievable how naturally everthing is in its place, in the salons, on the terraces, in the workshops and stables of the manor house Els Calderés near Sant Joan. Only a few years ago the aristocratic owners left their plush manor house and moved to their town palazzo in Palma. They left everything as it had been for centuries. Therefore the visitor has a genuine insight into the life on one of the about 500 autonomous country estates which are still on the island. For a long time they have no longer been economically profitable, and so the landed aristorcracy reconsider and change their partly imposing estates into hotels, restaurants, night clubs. Or into a museum like Els Calderés, from whose past as a wine estate the splendid wine cellar bears witness, as is the case with the huge granary on the top floor as a corn estate.

Sineu | Das Zentrum Mallorcas

39 Viele Wege führen nach Sineu. Das kleine Marktstädtchen liegt genau im geographischen Mittelpunkt Mallorcas. Das wusste auch ein mittelalterlicher Herrscher wie Jaime II. zu schätzen. Er baute sich in Sineu einen königlichen Palast, wo er oft residierte, um aufmüpfige Untertanen an die Kandare zu nehmen. Der steinerne Löwe an der Freitreppe zur Pfarrkirche Mare de Déu del Angels verweist auf den heiligen Markus, den Schutzpatron Sineus. Jeden Mittwoch steuern im Sommer Touristenbusse das Landstädtchen an, in das sich sonst wenige Urlauber verirren: Dann ist Markttag, und der läuft noch immer so wie vor 100 Jahren ab. Bauern und Händler bieten die Waren an; besonders intensiv wird um das Vieh gefeilscht.
Sineu ist auch unter den Freunden der mallorquinischen Küche ein Geheimtipp. Man isst gut, deftig und preiswert, eben bäuerlich, in den cellers (Kellerlokalen), etwa Frit mallorquí, ein Potpourri aus Lamm-Innereien, Sopes mallorquines (Kohltopf auf hauchdünnen Brotscheiben) oder porcella (Spanferkel). Dazu mundet ein einfacher roter Landwein.

The centre of Mallorca

Many roads lead to Sineu. The little market town is situated exactly in the geographic centre of Mallorca. That was already appreciated by a medieval ruler like Jaime II. In Sineu he built a royal palace where he often resided in order to take rebellious subjects in hand. The stone lion on the steps to the parish church Mare de Déu del Angels refers to St Mark, Sineu's patron saint. Every Wednesday in summer tourist buses head for the little country town. Then it is market day, and everything goes off exactly as it did 100 years ago. Farmers and tradesmen offer their goods: a lot of haggling is done over the livestock. Sineu is also an inside tip for friends of the Mallorcan cuisine. One eats good and solid food – simply rural – in the "cellers" (cellar restaurants). Frit mallorquí, a potpourri of lamb's offal, Sopes mallorquines, cabbage stew on thin pieces of bread, or porcella (sucking pig). With it goes a simple but genuine red local wine.

Puig de Randa | Tafelberg mit Tafelfreuden

40 Mit 542 Metern ist er die höchste Erhebung des Plà, der weiten Ebene in der Inselmitte. Und so ist der Tafelberg von allen Seiten weithin sichtbar. Er schützt das kleine Dorf Randa mit Kopfsteinpflastergassen und Gärten. Von dort fährt man die serpentinenreiche Bergstraße hinauf, die drei Klöster verbindet. Das unterste ist verlassen, klebt malerisch wie ein Schwalbennest im Sandsteinfels, an der sonnenbeschienenen Südseite des Berges. Das mittlere ist noch von Ordensbrüdern bewohnt; besichtigt werden kann nur seine kleine Kirche. Das Santuari de Nostra Senyora de Cura krönt das Ganze. Allerdings trüben Radarmasten auf der Gipfelplatte zunächst den Blick. Entschädigt werden Sie jedoch mit einem tollen Rundumblick über die ganze Insel. Und mit dem Gefühl, auf kulturgeschichtlich heiligem Boden zu stehen. Denn hierhin zog sich im Jahr 1263 Ramón Llull zurück, nachdem er, durch Visionen geläutert, seinem genusssüchtigen Leben am mallorquinischen Königshof entsagt hatte. Süchtig machen kann der (Kräuter-)Licor Randa, den es nur hier oben in der Klosterklause zu kaufen gibt!

Mesa with culinary delights

With 542 metres it is the highest elevation of the Plà, the wide plateau in the interior of the island. And it is visible from all sides from a long distance. It protects the little village Randa with cobblestone streets and gardens. From there, one ought to drive up the mountain road with many hairpin bends which connects three monasteries. The lowest is deserted, sticks picturesquely like a swallow's nest in the sandstone rock, on the sun-warmed south side of the mountain. The middle one is still inhabited by monks: only the little church can be visited. The Santuari de Nostra Senyora de Cura crowns everything. However, radar masts on the beak mar the view somewhat. You are compensated however by a super panorama over the whole island. And with the feeling of standing on culture-historical holy ground. For it was here that Ramón Llull retreated to in 1263 after having had visions and renouncing his life of excesses at the Mallorcan court. You can become addicted to the (herbal) Licor Randa, which can only be bought up here in the monastery hemitage.

S'Arenal |
Badespaß im Aqualand

Aqualand
Mai-Okt.
tgl. 10-18 Uhr

41 Hand in Hand und mit lautem Geschrei sausen kleine und große Kinder auf der "Kamikaze"-Riesenrutsche mit mehreren Buckeln und fast senkrechten Gleitspuren hinab ins kühle Nass. Dem Badespaß sind kaum Grenzen gesetzt im "Aqualand", dem größten von vier Wasserparks. Er liegt in der Nähe des Flughafens bei Arenal an der Autobahnausfahrt Nr. 13. Die "Cola de Diablo", der Teufelsschwanz, ist eine dunkle, gewundene Röhre, durch die man auf Gummiringen schießt, mit gehörigem Prickeln im Bauch. Ein Heidenspaß für die ganze Familie. Eine Attraktion jagt die nächste; insgesamt sind es 20 auf mehr als 200 000 Quadratmetern, vorwiegend begrünter Fläche. Und anscheinend gibt es auf einer vom Meer umgebenen Insel nichts Aufregenderes als ein gechlorter Riesenpool mit künstlichen Wellen; warum sonst herrscht gerade hier immer Hochbetrieb? Aber das gehört halt zu einer touristisch durch und durch strukturierten Insel, wie auch die Afrika-Auto-Safari bei Cala Major, Reptilienzoo und Kunst-Eisbahn (!) im "Festival Parc" bei Marratxí und die Papageien- und Delfin-Show im "Marineland" bei Portals Nous.

Bathing fun in Aqualand

Big and little children whiz hand in hand and screeching loudly on the "Kamikaze" giant slide with several bumps and almost vertical sliding tracks down into the cool water. There are no limits to the bathing fun in "Aqualand", the largest of four water parks. It is situated near the airport at Arenal on the Motorway Exit No. 13. The "Cola de Diablo", the Devil's Tail, is a dark, winding pipe through which one shoots on rubber tyres, with butterflies in one's tummy. It is terrific fun for the whole family. One attraction follows the next, there are 20 altogether in more than 200,000 m^2 mainly grassy area. And on the island surrounded by the sea there is apparently nothing more exciting than a huge chlorinated pool with artificial waves; why else should there always be high season here? But that's part of an island which is fixed up for tourists from beginning to end, as with the Africa-Auto-Safari near Cala Major, Reptile Zoo and Artificial Ice Rink (!) in the "Festival Parc" near Marratxi and the Parrot and Dolphin Show in "Marineland" near Portals Nous.

Pórtol | Ton in Ton

42 Die authentischen Tontöpfe sind rostbraun wie Mallorcas Erde, einseitig glasiert und heißen olles, wenn sie hoch und bauchig, und greixoneres, wenn sie flach sind. Noch immer kochen Hausfrauen in diesen irdenen Töpfen, noch immer werden sie in Insel-Töpfereien hergestellt. Natürlich längst mit Hilfe einer elektrisch angetriebenen Scheibe, und der Brennofen wird natürlich auch schon lange nicht mehr mit Mandelschalen geheizt. Aber immerhin leben einige Werkstätten noch vom Verkauf ihrer Töpfe. Größtes Töpferzentrum ist das kleine Dorf Pórtol nahe bei Santa Maria. Hier sind noch acht Töpferfamilien zuhause, denen man bei der Arbeit zuschauen darf und die ihre Ware direkt in Pórtol oder auf den Wochenmärkten und bei fires (Messen) verkaufen.
Eine traditionelle Handwerkskunst ist auch die Leineweberei. Noch gibt es zwei auf der Insel, "Bujosa" in Santa Maria und "Vicenc (mit cedé)" in Pollenca. Beide weben die robes de llengo, schwere Dekorations-Stoffe mit farbigem Zungenmuster, meist Ton in Ton. Das geschieht nach uralten, geheimgehaltenen Rezepturen, in Santa Maria noch in aufwändiger Handarbeit, in Pollenca schon maschinell.

Tone in tone

The authentic clay pots are rust-brown like Mallorca's soil, glazed on one side and are called "olles" when they are tall and bulbous and "greixoneres" when they are flat. Housewives still cook in these earthen pots and they are still produced in the island potteries. Of course, with the help of an electrically powered potter's wheel, and the kiln hasn't been heated with almond shells for a long time either. However, some workshops still live from selling their pottery. The largest pottery centre is the little village Pórtol near Santa Maria. Eight potter's families still live here, and one can watch them working. They sell their goods directly in Pórtol or at weekly market and "fires" (fairs). Linen weaving is another traditional craft. There are still two left on the island, "Bujosa" in Santa Maria and "Vincenç" in Pollença. Both weave the "robes de llengo", heavy decoration materials with coloured tongue patterns, mostly tone in tone. This is done according to ancient secret "recipes", in Santa Maria done in costly handmade work, in Pollença by machine.

4 Extra-Touren Special tours

Mallorca entdeckt und erlebt nur der wirklich, der sich bewegt: wie – das spielt letztlich keine Rolle. Wer will, schnürt die Wanderstiefel, packt ein Picknick in den Rucksack und folgt uralten Hirten-, Pilger- oder Schmugglerpfaden, hinauf in Mallorcas grandiose Bergwelt. Jedoch: markierte Wanderwege sind selten, ein Wanderführer ist ratsam. Ganze Gruppen buntbehoster, sportiver Radfahrer, die meist auf die Autorouten angewiesen sind, bevölkern in der kühleren Jahreszeit die Insel. Wer jedoch die ganze Vielfalt dieses Eilands auskosten möchte, mietet sich einen Wagen. Die meisten Highlights der Insel liegen im Bereich der Serra de Tramuntana, jenem Hochgebirgszug zwischen der Halbinsel Formentor im Norden und dem Hafen von Andratx im Südwesten. Kein Wunder, dass sich auf den kurvenreichen Bergstraßen nicht selten Autos, Ausflugsbusse, Motor- und Fahrräder in die Quere kommen. Nehmen sie sich also Zeit für Touren nach Formentor, Lluc, Sóller, Deià, Valldemossa, Banyalbufar, Estellencs und Andratx und genießen sie in Ruhe die atemberaubenden Ausblicke, die sich Ihnen immer wieder bieten.

You can only really explore and experience Mallorca if you move – and it is of no matter how. Those who want to put on their hiking boots, pack a picnic in their rucksacks and follow the old shepherds', pilgrims' or smugglers' paths up into Mallorca's magnificent mountain world. However, there are very few marked trails, so it is advisable to take a map of trails with you. Whole groups of colourfully-dressed sporty cyclists who are mostly dependent on auto routes populate the island in the cooler time of the year. However, those who want to make the most of the whole variety of this wonderful island should hire a car. Most of the highlights of the island are around the Serra de Tramuntana, that high mountain range between Formentor peninsula in the north and Andratx harbour in the south-west. It is no wonder that cars, excursion busses, motorbikes and cycles sometimes get in each other's way on the winding mountain roads. So take your time for tours to Formentor, Lluc, Sóller, Deià, Valldemossa, Banyalbufar, Estellencs and Andratx and in peace and quiet enjoy the breathtaking views which appear around every bend.

Tour 1 | Inca – Lluc – Sóller – Deià – Son Marroig – Valldemossa

Länge: 70 km
Dauer: Tagestour (ca. 8 Stunden)
Fahrt durchs Gebirge der Tramuntana, dort, wo Mallorca am höchsten und aufregendsten ist und entlang einer der schönsten Küstenstraßen Europas.

Von Inca geht's in Richtung Selva stetig bergan durch den "Raiguer", das Vorgebirgsland. Nach den beiden Dörfern Selva und Caimari beginnen die Serpentinen. Erste Rast könnte am Kloster Lluc sein. Es geht weiter in Richtung Sóller durch dunkle Steineichenwälder und vorbei an fantastischen Felsformationen. An den sogenannten "Miradors" (Aussichtspunkten) sollte man unbedingt parken und die tollen Ausblicke genießen! Nach dem letzten Tunnel geht's bergab ins Orangen-Tal von Sóller und wieder hinauf in Richtung Deià. Man parkt in Son Marroig (s. Abb.) und schaut auf die Halbinsel Sa Foradada. Etwa 5 km vor Valldemossa verlässt die Straße die Küste. Nach Besichtigung der Kartause und des blumengeschmückten Unterdorfes geht die Fahrt zurück zum Ferienort.

Length: 70 km
Duration: day tour (about 8 hours)
Tour through the mountains of the Tramuntana, where Mallorca is at its highest and most exciting, and along one of the most beautiful coastal roads in Europe.

From Inca you travel uphill towards Selva through the "Raiguer", the foothills. The winding roads start after the two villages Selva and Caimari. One can stop for a first break at Lluc Monastery. Go on towards Sóller through dark holm oak woods and past fantastic rock formations. One really ought to park at the so-called "Miradors" (viewpoints) and enjoy the fantastic views! After the last tunnel it goes downhill into the orange valley of Sóller and up again in the direction of Deià. Park in Son Marroig (see picture) and look onto the peninsula Sa Foradada. The road leaves the coast about 5 km before Valldemossa. After visiting the Carthusian monastery and the lower village decorated with flowers, one makes the journey back to the holiday resort.

Tour 2 | Mirador de ses Barques – Coll de Biniamar – Cala Tuent

Höhenunterschied: ca. 300 m
Dauer: 4,5 Stunden
Anstrengende Wanderung durch Olivenhaine und Eichenwälder mit aussichtsreichem Küstenweg zur Badebucht Cala Tuent.

Man fährt zum Parkplatz des Mirador des ses Barques an der C 710 Sóller-Pollenca. Nun geht es rechts zum Einstieg "Cala Tuent". Erst ein wenig bergauf und dann auf breiten Wegen nur noch bergab durch herrliche Olivenbaum-Terrassen, vorbei an zwei verfallenen Fincas, erreicht man nach 1 Std. im Talkessel die alte Finca Balitx d'Avall (s. Abb.). Nun folgt ein ermüdender Aufstieg auf einem Sonnenhang zum Coll de Biniamar (3/4 Std.). Oben angekommen führt der Weg zunächst ein wenig bergab und dann rechts immer oberhalb des Wassers entlang. Das alte Wasserwerk sa Costera, nach dem dieser Weg benannt ist, liegt unten links. Der schmale steinige Pfad führt 2,5 Std. durch Dißgras bergauf. Am Ende weisen Schilder hinunter zur Cala Tuent. Nach einer Badepause fährt man entweder mit dem Schiff (von sa Calobra um 16 Uhr) nach Port de Sóller zurück (ca. 3/4 Std. und dann mit dem Taxi vom Hafen zum Ausgangspunkt) oder man ruft ein Taxi, das zum Mirador de ses Barques zurückfährt.

Difference in altitude: about 300 m
Duration: 4,5 hours
Strenuous hike through olive groves and oak woods with a coastal path with good views to the bathing bay Cala Tuent.

Go to the car park of the Mirador de ses Barques on the C 710 Sóller – Pollença. Now turn right to the entry Cala Tuent". First go uphill a little and then along wide paths downhill through magnificent olive tree terraces, past two derelict fincas and after one hour one reaches the old finca Falitx d'Avall in the valley basin (see picture). Now there is a tiring climb on a sunny slope to the Col de Biniamar (3/4 hour). Once up there, the path first leads downhill a little, then right, always above the water. The old waterworks sa Costera, after which this path is named, lies at the bottom to the left. The small stony path leads uphill for 2 1/2 hours. At the end signs show down to Cala Tuent. After a bathing break you can either go back to Port de Sóller by boat (from sa Calobra at 4pm), about 3/4 hour and then by taxi from the harbour to the starting-point, or call a taxi which takes you back to the Mirador de ses Barques.

Tour 3 | Inca – Port de Pollenca – Formentor – Alcúdia – Inca

Länge: 110 km
Dauer: Tagestour (ca. 8 Std.)
Rundfahrt durch vorwiegend flaches Land und über die bergige Halbinsel Formentor.

Vom Ausgangsort Inca führt die C 713 in Richtung Alcúdia. Man folgt dem Schild "Coves de Campanet" und besichtigt die Tropfsteinhöhle. Nun geht es in Richtung Pollenca. Dort besucht man den Kalvarienberg (s. Abb.). Auf der kurvenreichen Passstraße in Richtung Formentor parkt man am Mirador (Aussichtspunkt), staunt und fährt in Richtung Cap Formentor. Vor dem Hotel Formentor lädt der Strand Cala Pi zu einem Besuch. Die Fahrt geht weiter in Richtung Cap Formentor: man hält kurz vor dem Tunnel und schaut links hinab auf die türkisblaue Bucht Cala Figuera. Am Kap selbst ist nur ein Leuchtturm zu sehen und kein Parkplatz zu finden! Deshalb fährt man denselben Weg, jedoch mit anderen Ausblicken, zurück nach Port de Pollenca und an der Hafenbucht entlang in Richtung Alcúdia. Vorbei an der S'Horta de sa Pobla geht es zurück nach Inca.

Length: 110 km
Duration: day tour (about 8 hours)
Round trip through mainly flat landscape and over the mountainous peninsula Formentor.

From the starting-point Inca the C 713 leads in the direction of Alcúdia. Follow the sign "Coves de Campanet" and visit the stalactite cave. Now take the direction towards Pollença. There you can visit calvary (see picture). On the winding pass towards Formentor Park at the Mirador (viewpoint), enjoy the view and drive on towards Cap Formentor. The beach Cala Pi in front of Hotel Formentor is very inviting. The journey goes on towards Cap Formentor: take a short break before the tunnel and look down to the left onto the turquoise bay Cala Figuera. At the cape itself, only a lighthouse is to be seen, and there is no car park! For that reason, return the same way, but with different views, to Port de Pollença and along the harbour bay towards Alcúdia. Travel back to Inca past the S'Horta de sa Pobla.

Tour 4 | Ermita de la Victoria – Mirador de Penya Rotja – Talaia d' Alcúdia

4

Länge: ca. 7 km
Dauer: 3,5 Std.,ca. 200 m Höhenunterschied
Mittelschwere Wanderung auf Wald- und Schotterwegen und auf steinigen Pfaden mit herrlichen Ausblicken auf Küste und Meer.

Ausgangspunkt ist der Parkplatz an der Ermita de la Victoria auf der gleichnamigen Halbinsel im Norden. Man startet am oberhalb gelegenen Forstweg, der stetig bergauf führt. Nach ca. 25 Min. geht links ein schmaler Bergpfad mit verwittertem Geländer ab. Der Steig wird immer felsiger und führt hoch über der Küste in Richtung Norden. Kurz vor dem Mirador klettert man durch die Öffnung eines ehemaligen Wehrturmes und folgt dem schmalen Pfad eng am Felsen und über dem Abgrund; Ketten und Gitter geben Halt. Nach 1 Std. erreicht man den Mirador de Penya Rotja (354 m) mit umwerfenden Ausblicken (s. Abb.). Nach einer Rast geht es denselben Weg zurück, bis zum breiten Forstweg, dem man nach links folgt. Er führt zum Sattel Coll d'es Pedregaret. Nach ca. 20 Min. erreicht man über eine Serpentinen-Trasse den Gipfel des Talaia d'Alcúdia (445 m). Ein fantastischer Rundblick belohnt den schweißtreibenden Aufstieg.

Length: about 7 km
Duration: 3,5 hours, about 200 m difference in altitude
Relatively difficult hike along forest and gravel paths and on stony paths with magnificent views of the coast and sea.

Starting-point is the car park at the Ermita de la Victoria on the peninsula of the same name in the north. Start at the higher forest path which constantly leads uphill. After about 25 minutes a small mountain path with weathered railings leads down to the left. The track gets more rocky and leads high up over the coast towards the north. Just before the Mirador you climb through the opening of a former watch-tower and follow the narrow path close to the cliff and over the precipice; chains and grating give support. After 1 hour you reach the Mirador de Penya Rotja (354 m) with fantastic views (see picture). After a break you return the same way till you reach the wide forest path and follow it to the left. It is partly signposted and leads to the saddle Coll d'es Pedregaret. After about 20 minutes you reach the summit of the Talaia d'Alcúdia (445 m) over a steeper winding marked route. A fantastic panoramic view rewards one for the arduous climb.

Impressum

Bildnachweis

Titelbild: Bildagentur Huber/Kreder
Fotos Ausflugziele: Bildagentur Huber/R. Schmid (Aufmacherfoto);
HB Verlag/H. Schwarzbach Nr. 6, 8, 10, 17, 18, 20, 21, 27, 28, 33 + 36;
P. M. Nahm Nr. 3, 12, 16, 19 + 39; R. Lewandowski Nr. 2, 4, 11 + 37;
R. Schenk-Kern Nr. 31; alle übrigen Fotos P. Rossbach
Fotos Extra-Touren: Bildagentur Huber/Kreder (Aufmacherfoto);
P. Rossbach S. 50-53

Impressum

Allianz Freizeitführer
© 2008 MAIRDUMONT GmbH & Co. KG, Ostfildern
Redaktion: MAIRDUMONT GmbH & Co. KG, Radegunde Schenk-Kern,
Marco-Polo-Zentrum, D-73760 Ostfildern, Tel. 0711/4502-0, Fax 0711/4502-1006
E-Mail: r.schenk-kern@mairdumont.com
Konzeption und Texte: Petra Rossbach
Übersetzung: Pauline Hejl
Kartografie: MAIRDUMONT GmbH & Co. KG, Ostfildern
Gestaltung: red.sign, Stuttgart
Layout: Studio Lang, Ostfildern

Die Angaben in diesem Freizeitführer, insbesondere die Anschriften und Öffnungszeiten, wurden sorgfältig geprüft. Für die Richtigkeit der Angaben kann trotzdem keine dauerhafte Gewähr übernommen werden.
Das Werk einschließlich aller seiner Teile ist urheberrechtlich geschützt. Jede urheberrechtsrelevante Verwertung ist ohne Zustimmung des Verlages unzulässig und strafbar. Das gilt insbesondere für Vervielfältigungen, Übersetzungen, Nachahmungen, Mikroverfilmungen und die Einspeicherung und Verarbeitung in elektronischen Systemen.